1
West of England

2
South East and East Midlands

3
Wales and West Midlands

4
North of England

5
Central and South Scotland

6
North of Scotland

Individual courses, prefixed by their regional numbers, are listed in the Contents under five categories: Seaside links; Parkland courses; Woodland courses; Riverside courses and Urban courses – an easy way to select your ideal green.

# A WORD OF THANKS

This edition published 1992 by the Promotional Reprint Company
Limited for Bookmart Limited, Desford Road, Enderby, Leicester, UK.

Printed and bound in Hong Kong.

ISBN 1 85648 047 X

# JUST A WORD

## BY DICKIE HENDERSON

Golf, in my humble opinion is the greatest game in the world, for many reasons. It sorts out the good sports from the bad, the timid from the bold, the fighter from the quitter, the honest man from the dishonest, the humourless from the humorous, in other words, the men from the boys. It is without doubt the world's greatest sporting freemasonry. For wherever you may find yourself anywhere in the world, should the subject of golf enter the conversation, in no time an invitation will be extended to play at the local golf club. Be it Sydney, Australia; Sunningdale, Berkshire or Scunthorpe, invariably the hospitality will be returned at your home course, and a worldwide network of lasting friendships will be cemented.

Golf is one of the only major sports where you are able to tread the same venues as have the greatest. To set foot on the centre court at Wimbledon for the avid tennis buff or the turf at Wembley Stadium for the soccer fan is just a dream, but for the golfer to walk the same greens and fairways, walked by Bobby Jones, Jack Nicklaus, Arnold Palmer, Gary Player and Tony Jacklin is not a dream, because for a normal green fee anyone who can swing a club can play Gleneagles, Pebble Beach, Wentworth and countless other famous courses and links.

Golf, barring bad luck or ill health, is an almost ageless game, whereas in the majority of competitive games the young man will almost always beat the older man. In golf, thanks to the handicapping system, the two fight it out on equal terms, with the old gentleman usually coming out the victor, as experience has made it possible for him to withstand the pressure when it mattered. I remember well that some years ago at Parkstone Golf Club in Bournemouth, a fourball played every morning and their

combined ages were three hundred and twenty-one years – needless to say that one day one of the four dropped dead, but for a golfer 'what a way to go'.

With the golfing explosion we now have the added attraction of Pro-Am tournaments, which gives the amateur the privilege of actually playing with the golfing giants. They now find themselves striding the fairways with and getting a few tips from their idols. A special kind of Pro-Am tournament held these days is Pro-Celebrity Golf as seen on television. It is not always as polished as it looks. Once, when I was playing with Billy Casper, a crowd of people were near the first tee. As I nervously teed up the ball, I suggested to a lady in the crowd that she was standing in an unsafe place. Amidst laughter, I made a terrific hit at the ball, which struck the unfortunate lady in the mouth. Fortunately she wasn't hurt. I reckon it was the best shot I played all day!

I myself will be forever grateful to the gentleman who introduced me to the Royal and Ancient game of Golf. I thank him because of its challenge. I thank him for the friends I have through golf, and I thank him because of the memories I cherish of Spring and Autumn mornings – the early frosts, the Autumn tints that have left an indelible picture in my mind of being a little bit closer to heaven. When you have read and inwardly digested the descriptions of the glorious courses detailed in this book, whether novice or old hand, you will be inspired to spend even more of your time battling on the green.

*Dickie Henderson*

# CONTENTS
## AND REGIONAL MAP

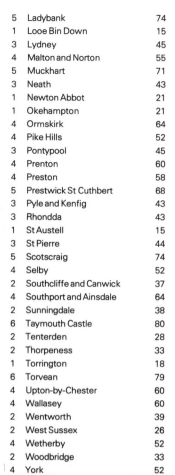

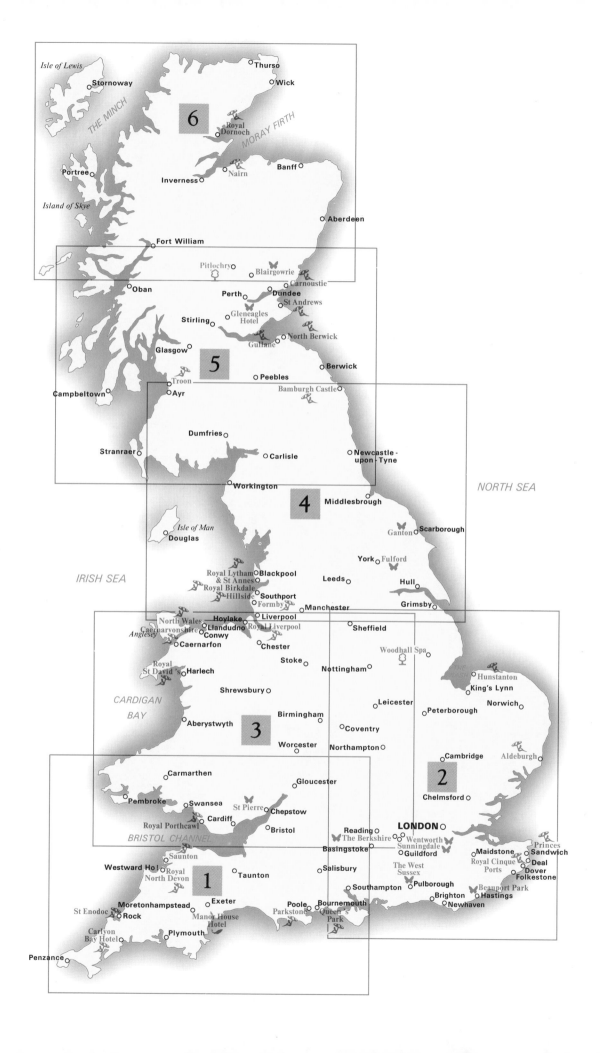

Isle of Lewis

Stornoway

THE MINCH

6

Thurso
Wick

Royal Dornoch

MORAY FIRTH

Portree

Island of Skye

Nairn
Banff

Inverness

Aberdeen

Fort William

Pitlochry
Blairgowrie

Oban

Carnoustie
Perth
Dundee
St Andrews

Gleneagles Hotel

Stirling

North Berwick
Gullane

Glasgow

5

Peebles

Berwick

Troon
Ayr

Bamburgh Castle

Campbeltown

Dumfries

Stranraer

Carlisle

Newcastle-upon-Tyne

Workington

4

Middlesbrough

NORTH SEA

Isle of Man

Douglas

Ganton
Scarborough

York
Fulford

Royal Lytham & St Annes
Blackpool

Leeds

Hull

IRISH SEA

Royal Birkdale
Hillside
Southport
Formby
Manchester

Grimsby

Hoylake
Liverpool

North Wales
Llandudno
Royal Liverpool

Sheffield

Caernarvonshire
Conwy

Chester

Anglesey
Caernarfon

Woodhall Spa

Royal St David's
Harlech

Stoke

Nottingham

THE WASH
Hunstanton
King's Lynn
Norwich

CARDIGAN BAY

Shrewsbury

Leicester

Peterborough

Aberystwyth

3

Birmingham

Coventry

Worcester

Northampton

Cambridge
Aldeburgh

Carmarthen

Gloucester

2

Pembroke
Swansea
St Pierre
Chepstow

Chelmsford

Royal Porthcawl
Cardiff

Bristol

BRISTOL CHANNEL

Reading
The Berkshire
Basingstoke

LONDON
Wentworth
Sunningdale
Guildford

Princes
Sandwich

Saunton

Maidstone

Deal

Westward Ho!
Royal North Devon

1

Taunton

Salisbury

The West Sussex

Royal Cinque Ports
Dover
Folkestone

Southampton
Pulborough

Beauport Park
Hastings

St Enodoc
Moretonhampstead
Rock

Exeter

Poole
Parkstone

Bournemouth
Queen's Park

Brighton
Newhaven

Carlyon Bay Hotel

Manor House Hotel

Plymouth

Penzance

# Location Map

Scale : 45 miles to 1 inch

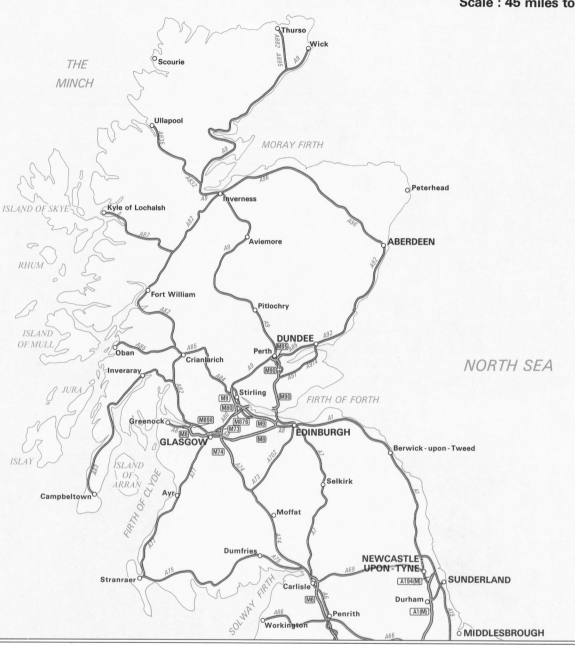

## Symbols used on location plans

| Symbol | Description | Symbol | Description | Symbol | Description |
|---|---|---|---|---|---|
| M3 S | Motorway | | Angling | † | Church |
| | Motorway under construction | | Riverside course | ✳ | Gardens, Parks |
| | Primary route | | Parkland course | ✗ | Windmill |
| | 'A' road | | Woodland course | 🏛 | Manor, Museum, House, Hall |
| | 'B' road | | Seaside links | | Priory, Abbey |
| | Unclassified | | Urban course | | |
| A40 | Road number | | Castle | | |

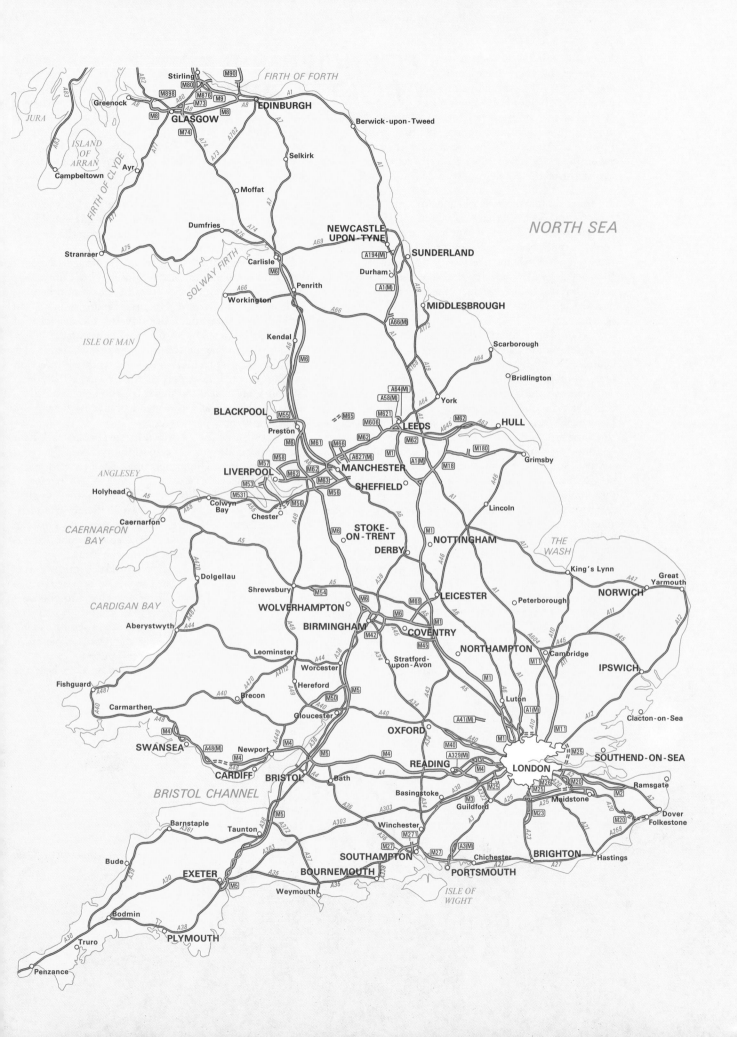

# TOUJOURS LA POLITESSE!

On the golf course there is no confusion between Gentlemen and Players – they should be one and same thing. If your handicap is a lack of gamesmanship finesse rather than a deficiency of playing skill, here is a guide to some of the finer points of the Royal and Ancient's rules – and some that the sport's governing body never came to terms with! Compared with most of the popular sports indulged in by leisure – hungry Britons, golf certainly has no surfeit of rules. Just forty-one of them are laid down by that august body of the Royal and Ancient Golf Club. This is not a lot to control a sport that is fought out over such varied courses, among a set of hazards that are more often akin to Acts of God than a designer's fancy and by a set of players whose ability varies from sporting loser to close to Bisley standards.

A former captain of the Royal and Ancient, Lord Brabazon of Tara, declared that 'Golf is too good a game to be messed around with'. He meant, of course, that the game could be spoilt by a more rigorous rule book which, if the more conservative members of golf's ruling body had their way, would include considerable restrictions on the way players should conduct themselves. His was a guarded reference to the unwritten laws of golfing etiquette.

His Lordship had very fixed ideas about what he saw as the deterioration of standards of behaviour on the golf courses. His bugbear was the tournament spectator. He once vent his feelings on a crowd. In a Match Play Tournament, the noisy partisans supporting Tony Jacklin in his stand against Gary Player were treated to: 'Good Heavens! You're like a football mob. Soon you'll be throwing toilet rolls!'.

Etiquette is never mentioned as part of the game of football, it does not feature in all-in wrestling and it has only occasionally intruded in the game of tennis; but the term 'golf etiquette' has been familiar for centuries. In fact golf may be the one game that becomes more fun when played to the rules of decorum. It is not the inbred politeness of the landed gentry that once held such great sway in the game – it is a matter of instinctive good manners and commonsense which can make the game that much more enjoyable. Take cheating, for example.

Hiccoughing while a rival is putting or sneezing on the tee when a player is at the top of his stroke are outright breaches of golf's unwritten rules. Slightly more subtle, none-the-less distracting at tense moments, and equally outrageous are pipe-lighting, club rattling and walking ahead of your opponent. Here the fine line must be drawn between outright distraction and the psychological approach. There is no reason at all why one should not mention the fall in his company's share quotation or some other *bête noire* on the walks to the tees.

Experts and professionals are not free from distractions either. Lee Trevino has made himself a little unpopular among the tight-knit circus of world-class players because he jokes with the crowd. His sin is talking too much in general, in total abandon of etiquette. One member of Royal Mid-Surrey was an outstandingly popular player despite being a poor performer. Everyone wanted to play with him because he had a longstanding throat infection which rendered him speechless and he was partially deaf. At golf a great deal too much is said about too little – between the tee and the green politeness demands a respectful silence.

Cheating is not necessarily restricted to players. Under the rules you also have a responsibility to see that your caddie plays fair. The professional, Maurice Bembridge discovered this to his cost in the 1968 PGA Championship when his caddie 'found' a ball and it went into play. Later, another ball turned up, which Bembridge identified as his, and the caddie admitted dropping a spare in the rough. He was sacked on the spot. Bembridge immediately disqualified himself from the game.

Caddies seldom cheat, however; and they are, unfortunately, a dying race. The days are long past when a touring golfer could drop in at any club and choose a caddie. In those few oases, like Walton Heath and Wentworth, where there are still some senior caddies retained, it is well worth hiring one for the experience, and for the experiences that he can impart.

Of course the majority of players have to bear the

burden of their own bag on a caddy cart or over the shoulder. There is form to be observed here, too. Never drop your club set to the ground with a crash, however exasperated you are becoming – it is rude, damages the clubs and, on the green, can scar sacred turf. Wheeled caddies can also damage turf unless used with care.

Perhaps the greatest crises of conscience and comportment occur when you are playing your marriage partner. Husband and wife must, at the very least, pretend to take an interest in each other's game. The olive branch of 'Good shot' or 'Hard luck' costs nothing and does much to smooth the run home from the club or for holidaying families, save the fortnight. The greatest concession of all that you can make is to ask your partner's advice on a particularly difficult lie.

One does not have to make such concessions to partners with whom you have only a casual relationship. If you really want to be generous and give your opponent a shortish putt, you can concede – but use it as a bargaining counter later in the game if at all possible. If you really do expect him to play a shot on which he is plainly craving a concession, be steadfast and utter not a word. If you slice a shot into the trees, content yourself with a single mild oath, whether you or your opponent is in trouble.

Try not to bore your opponent by playing at a snail's pace. This is not a permitted ploy of golf gamesmanship – and do not hinder those following you round the course. Loss of a ball may mean they catch up with you anyway. Invite them to play through, and stifle your impulse to mutter, 'What's the damned rush?'.

Quite the most controversial area of all which the Royal and Ancient must be reluctant to tackle, is the matter of dress on the course. One of many golf anomalies is that male players often look sloppier (or more casual!) in the clubhouse than when out on the greens. The vogue for dazzling jockey caps, tartan trews, two-tone cashmere cardigans and psychedelic shoes, came, along with other excesses in the game, relatively recently. Doug Sanders once arrived to play the Open with a pair of patent leather shoes in a variety of hues to match his ensemble – a different one each day. It was only a matter of time before other clubmen began to follow suit. Gentlemen players should take a lead from

the chic and eminent sensibility shown by lady players, who have stood aloof from this coquettish display.

Clothing has been a debating point throughout golf's history. In *The Complete Golfer* the great Harry Vardon wrote: 'Always use braces in preference to a belt . . . when a man plays in a belt he has an unaccustomed sense of looseness, and his shoulders are too much beyond control.' Nobody today would place very much emphasis on this stricture. However, there do remain those clubs in Britain which have never allowed standards or waistbands to slip. Jackets will always be worn in the hallowed precincts of St Andrews and Muirfield – other fortresses of sartorial rectitude include Prestwick, Troon and Sunningdale.

Some clubs have made an attempt to control dress in the clubhouse. Cricketer Tom Graveney, a persevering low-handicap golfer, once made his entry into Cirencester Golf Club attired in his County Captain's cricket blazer, meticulously adjusted MCC tie, and underpants. He had read the varnished sign at the door of the locker-room – 'Be Properly Dressed – Wear Jackets and Ties'!

Punctuality is the essence of golf etiquette. While few players will be as unlucky as American professional Johnny Bulla, who was disqualified from a national tournament for starting too *early*, a prompt arrival at the tee should be a priority. Archie Compston was struck out of an American Open for arriving five minutes late after a tardy connection on a journey of over 3000 miles. Unluckiest latecomer of all was the Amateur Championship competitor who thought his train from Ayr stopped at Prestwick. As the train hurtled non-stop past the first tee, he yelled to the Starter from his carriage window that he would be back as soon as possible. He was disqualified.

Finally, the player has to know how to behave at the most rigorous hole of all. Let there be no dispute about it – the *winner* buys the first round. This is fortunately likely to be the cheapest one of all, as only a cad would take anything dearer than a beer. Later rounds of spirits are reserved for those players with apologies to make for any falls from grace that may have become apparent, because in golf the most gilded rule of all is that if you do stray from the path of righteousness, never get caught.

Everybody has those off days when not a shot goes right for hole after hole and the putter seems possessed of a mind of its own. If troubles persist, you may be making some of golf's fundamental mistakes. Most of the worst faults can creep into your play long after you think you have mastered the techniques. Suddenly you could find you are being plagued by errors which could be due to a faulty grip, an awkward stance when

# PLAY BETTER GOLF

addressing the ball, or – most common of all – insufficient care and over-confidence in making the swing or controlling the putt.

Before you can hope to find the cure, it is important first to recognise the problems. That demands an almost ruthless self-analysis of your play. The advice given here will help to clear the path to your development of a fluidity and style that will be the envy of your partners.

## Getting a grip

It may be the first thing that many players learn – the grip. It is equally easy to forget after a short period away from the game or during the excitement of playing your first few games and perfecting a swing. The grip is, after all, a mechanical joint between the muscle and lever action of the body, transmitted through the arms, and the amplification this gains in the lever of the club. It is not just a question of white knuckles and attempts to crush the handle. It is a joint that must have balanced flexibility allowing for added acceleration of the swing, some absorption of the shock of hitting the ball and thereby a fluid follow-through. While the grip of the left hand should never vary, some control over the tension applied by the right hand is required, especially when playing woods.

Most players will have been taught to use the Vardon or overlapping grip which has the advantage of holding four fingers of the left hand in contact with the shaft. The alternatives are the 'base-ball' and 'interlocking' grips popular among a few star players – these may suit some newcomers to the game but they are broadly more suitable to a highly developed style of play.

In the Vardon grip, the left hand should hold the club

half an inch from the top – the club should lie across the lowest finger joints and the most pressure should be exerted by the last two fingers. To complete the grip, place the right hand below the left in a half-clenched position and interlock the two hands by putting the little finger of the right hand over the index finger of the left. The right thumb should then fall naturally over the left thumb. The Vs formed by the thumb and index finger of each hand should be in line with the shaft for most players and between two and three knuckles of the left hand should be visible. There is no shame in checking this at every tee until you confidently adopt the correct grip by habit.

## Swing right

Far from being the apparently simple action of actually hitting the ball, the swing is an orchestrated set of muscle movements which involve all the major muscles of the body and a few minor ones too. Get one wrong and it will be a long time before you get back to the clubhouse.

Your stance should evenly distribute your body weight between the two feet which should be about as far apart as your shoulders. The toes should be in a line *parallel* to the direction of the shot. Bend the knees very slightly as

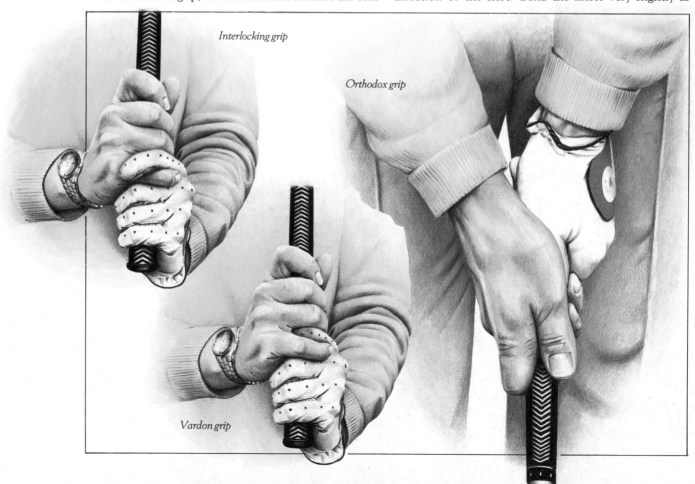

Interlocking grip

Orthodox grip

Vardon grip

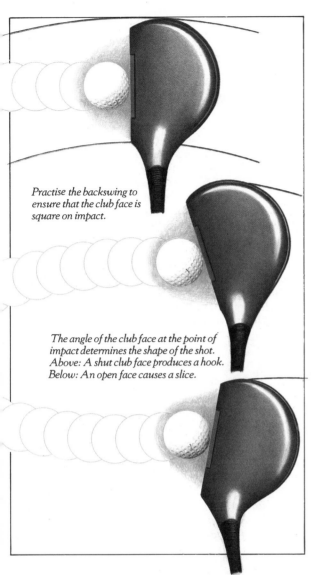

*Practise the backswing to ensure that the club face is square on impact.*

*The angle of the club face at the point of impact determines the shape of the shot. Above: A shut club face produces a hook. Below: An open face causes a slice.*

On the downswing, it is the muscles of the left arm, aided to a certain extent by the right hand, that transmit the energy to the ball. Never tense the right wrist, since the smooth transmission of the flow of the downswing depends on wrist flexibility, and tensing the right wrist can also distort the open-shut presentation of the club face. The action of the wrists, trailing behind that of the left arm muscles for the first half of the downswing, comes into play in the last 90° before impact with the ball. During the downswing the left heel will regain contact with the ground at an early stage so once again the body weight is evenly distributed on both feet, particularly at the moment of impact.

Follow through in a mirror image of the downswing with the body weight shifting on to the left foot and the right heel being raised. As you apply a braking action to the motion, there will be a tendency for the right knee to close in on the left leg and the arms may go a little higher in response to the momentum of the swing.

### An open or shut case

The angling of the wrists during the swing dictate the angle at which the club face will be presented to the ball. How this affects flight is discussed below in the case of the hook and the slice. The main point to stress here is that the left wrist should be at such an angle to the arm that the club grip is close to a line drawn along the centre of the forearm. Setting the palm and fingers above that line tends to open the club face – below the line the club face may be shut at presentation.

### The eyes have it

It cannot be stressed too much that the eyes must be glued to the ball throughout the swing and fully into the follow-through. This advice applies to all types of shot including the putt. Part of the reason is that to keep the head still aids balance allowing you to complete the swing in full control of your muscle movements. It is the concentration on the ball that enables you to fully regulate what happens at the point of impact as well. However the head will have to move in the last stage of the follow-through so the right arm is not obstructed.

### Club selection

Far too often players are tempted to base the club selection on the maximum range required of a shot. This implies the use of maximum power in the swing and it is at this peak of effort that most players will have substantially less control. Select an iron with longer range and you will be able to keep the effort required for the shot in the middle range of your abilities which offers that much more possibility of control.

### Teeing the ball

Many drives are ruined by a simple mistake in teeing the ball. The ball should be at such a height that some half of the ball is above the face of the wood. It should be to the left of a line drawn through the centre of your stance but not quite as far over as the left heel.

### Slicing

A tendency to slice can be compounded from many factors but by far the most common result of a mistake in address or stance is that the club face is moved across the ball at impact. Equally, the club face may be at an open

though you are about to sit down on a high stool. Your arms should not be tensed in an extended position – rather, you should aim to have a natural fall of the arm from the shoulder with a very slight curve to the spine. In the swing position, check again that the weight is evenly distributed on your feet – most weight should fall on the balls of the feet when driving.

Address the ball in this stance and with the club face square to the ball, start the backswing – but only by a foot or so. This is the limit of combined arm and wrist movement without shoulder movement. Practise this a few times, checking that each time you return to the ball the club is square to it.

Now tee the ball correctly, walk away a few paces and then back to adopt the stance and address the ball – if you do not find that your stance is relaxed, just as it was before, at the correct address relax and attempt it again.

During the backswing, ensure that your left shoulder does not fall. The whole action should be one of a pivot in which the pelvis, the spine and the shoulder blade all add their degrees of flexibility and rotation. Naturally, at the top of the swing the right elbow falls and some of the weight will have shifted off the left foot allowing for a slight rise. Do not allow the stance of the right leg to change at all. The tendency is for the hip to drop but at all costs one must resist it.

11

angle. Spin imparted to the ball can cause it to swerve and the misdirection of the open face seals the drive's fate. First check your stance to see that it is parallel to the line of flight. A slightly open stance could be the problem. You can use stance to overcome a tendency to slice. By closing the stance – drawing back the right foot a little from the parallel line – you drive an intentional hook because this creates an in-to-out swing. Hopefully the degree of hook cancels the degree of slice.

These measures will often remedy what is the prime cause of the slice, the tendency to pull the arms in towards the body shortly before the moment of impact in the hope of giving the ball more lift. The fact is that if the ball is correctly hit in the first place it will have all the lift that is required.

An open club face at the point of impact is the other main problem. Practice your grip and then the swing, checking your wrist position and then checking that the face comes down square to the ball at the point of impact.

A false form of the slice is when the ball is pushed off line by a failure to follow-through correctly. This can only be cured by dogged swing practice.

### The hook

Hooking is usually thought of as the bane of the professional golfer as the developed style of the in-to-out swing creates the possibility of a left swerve, especially if the club face is closed. As with the slice, the first thing to check is the stance. If with a parallel stance you still find that you are hooking, you may be able to apply a measure of correction by withdrawing the left foot from the parallel line to create an out-to-in swing.

It is far more likely, however, that you are presenting a closed face to the ball. Check your grip – you may well find that you have three knuckles of the left hand fully in view. You can open the face of the club at address by adjusting the grip to show only two knuckles.

The fault can also lie on the back-swing. Any tendency to pull the club sharply upwards with the right hand dominating the effort tends to close the face of the club at the top of the swing. You must develop a swing in which the left hand controls the movement of the back-swing.

### Topping the ball

Like slicing, the common fault of topping can be caused by a player too eager to loft the ball into the air. It may

result from hitting the top of the ball during the down swing. At least as frequently it is quite the reverse of this – it occurs because the club is already on its way off the ground before the moment of impact. Very often the topped shot is the result of a shift in the arc of the swing either by a change in the angle of the left knee or by a right dip of the shoulder. Both faults can frequently be observed.

Skying is the opposite of topping and results from the same shift of the arc of swing to the extent that the ball may not be hit by the club face at all. In wood shots the skyed ball will quite probably have been hit by the upper edge of the club. In iron shots, contact with the lower half of the ball is the problem, particularly with an open face at impact.

### Shanking or socketing

These are the terms for a shot hit with the socket part of the club head instead of the face. It happens to everybody at some stage and may never assume the proportions of a serious fault. If it does, however, the cure must be quick.

It has often been considered that shanking may result from a overpowerful action of the right arm in the swing producing something of a bend in the left arm at the point of impact.

The left arm must always be straight at this point. It can also be the result of lifting the head too early in an anxious search for the flight of the ball. Keep the head down and concentrate fully on the ball.

### Grounding the club

Sometimes called sclaffing, the fault of grounding the club head behind the ball tends to impart considerable spin to the ball, not unlike that of topping. It is, of course, the result of lowering the arc of the swing, a fault that may arise from a knee-bend or, more usually, a drop of the right shoulder during the down-swing.

### Putting problems

The putting grip is just as important as the driving grip and should be practiced just as assiduously. In this grip the palms of the hand face each other, the left hand thumb falls under the right hand thumb muscle and the hands are interlocked only to the extent that the first finger of the left hand is placed over the closed fingers of the right. This grip permits a certain amount of wrist flexibility with equal emphasis to each hand.

While there are many players who have had success with the stabbing form of putt, which imparts energy to the ball in a short, sharp, tapping swing with very little follow-through, most beginners will gain more confidence by the development of a disciplined and controlled swing and follow-through.

The ball should be addressed at a position a little further forward than normal on a line from the left heel. The head and the body must be kept perfectly still. You should now find that the left hand is naturally in a straight line with the forearm at the address. As the putter is swung back, the wrists are permitted to move to the extent that the putter comes roughly in line with the forearm. Bring the putter down in line with a deliberate action of the arms in unison, such that in the follow-through the left wrist and the putter are still in line with the arm.

There is absolutely no substitute for repeated practice in developing your putting style.

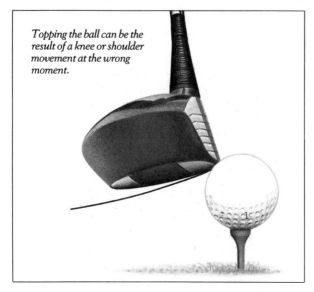

*Topping the ball can be the result of a knee or shoulder movement at the wrong moment.*

# Carlyon Bay

Carlyon Bay Hotel, St Austell,
Cornwall
*Tel: Par (072 681) 4250*

1 mile west of St Blazey on A390
Seaside/parkland course: 6501yds,
SSS71
*Course designer:* J Hamilton Stutt

Visitors welcome – telephone in
advance
*Professional:* A J Malcolm

Hotels: Carlyon Bay Hotel (owner of
the Carlyon Bay Course), St Austell
*Tel: Par (072 681) 2304*
(78 rm) located 100yds from course

Porth Avallen Hotel★★★ Carlyon Bay
*Tel: Par (072 681) 2802*
(26rm)
Closed mid December – mid January

there is the spice of danger in the close proximity to the cliff edge – risk of losing the ball of course, not to life and limb. The edge is a physical factor and a mental intrusion at the first two holes and the 6th, 7th and 9th.

Nature has provided most of the facilities for golf here and that makes it an exacting course. Starting eastward across the cliffs it has some heady slopes and climbs – often it is the run-off of the land to the sea that demands very accurate tee shots.

Outstanding holes on the outward leg are the 4th and the 9th. The 4th is an excellent par 5 as J Hamilton Stutt's design turns inland with the railway to the left of the fairway. Considerable length is required to clear a great grass bank cutting across the sight line. Pulling clear

for those who fail to make it will cost dearly.

The 9th turns back again and although it is only some 330 yards in length, there is the slope to contend with. An unusual feature for the unwary is a deep grass pit immediately in front of the green, matched by a further hollow on the other side to snare the over-enthusiastic swinger. In contrast, the 10th is a swing into the sky to make headway down the slope, over 500 yards to what seems like the level of the beach. This is the furthest point from the hotel – and the nearest to the great white mounds of the china clay works which are such a prominent feature of the St Austell skyline.

It takes two holes to regain the heights of Carlyon Bay's cliff. The 11th is short at about 170 yards and the 12th follows the same uphill

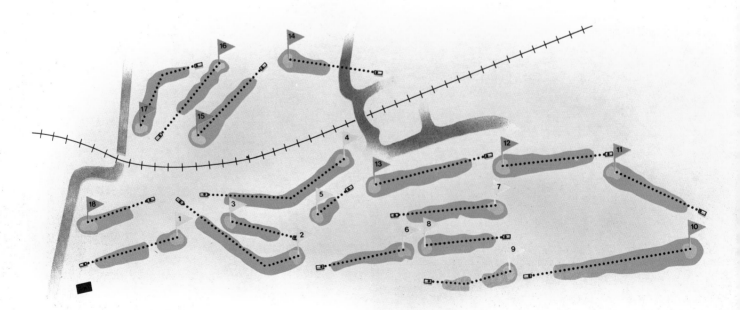

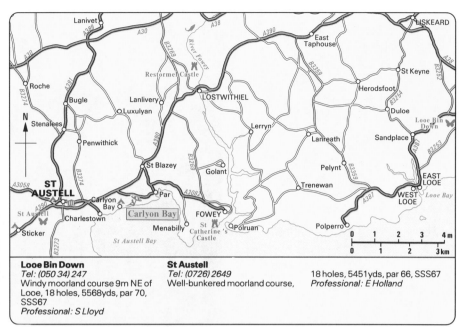

**Looe Bin Down**
*Tel: (050 34) 247*
Windy moorland course 9m NE of
Looe, 18 holes, 5568yds, par 70,
SSS67
*Professional: S Lloyd*

**St Austell**
*Tel: (0726) 2649*
Well-bunkered moorland course,

18 holes, 5451yds, par 66, SSS67
*Professional: E Holland*

line. This prepares you for the challenge of the 13th, an impressive par 5 of more than 500 yards sloping to the right all the way – place yourself accurately to the left and you will still have to contend with its elevated green.

By clever arrangement, Carlyon's character changes here to that of parkland golf as the course crosses the railway for four holes of a very interesting quality. Par 4 may seem within a visitor's scope on the medium-length 14th until he views the bunkers invitingly placed to the left and right of the green. From here, hole 15 takes a wicked uphill dogleg to the right around a copse. Survive that and the green is right next to the railway with only a few feet of rough marking the divide.

The same sort of form marks the 17th – 380 yards of rising ground with a dogleg and a wickedly bunkered green set against a tree-fringed bank. Fascination is held to the end by the final hole which features both road and railway out of bounds – and all in 200 yards.

One of the attractions of Carlyon Bay, de-servedly the home of county golf in Cornwall, is that the course is so open and inviting. Where the skill comes in is gauging your plac-ings, as the bunkers are skilfully designed, flat and unseen to the visitor picking a way round the course for the first time. Flat they might be, but they place a very high premium on accu-racy at all times.

These days Cornwall's chief source of in-come is derived from thousands of holidaymak-ers attracted to its magnificent coastline and picturesque country villages. It was not always the case. The Duchy was known for its tin and copper mining, seafaring and, notably, fish-ing. Reminders of these hard times are housed in an 18th-century boatbuilder's workshop at Mevagissey's Folk Museum. This quaint fish-ing village – which has retained its reputation as an offshore angler's paradise, becomes choked with sightseers in high season and car parking space is limited. Those unable to get to see the Model Railway Museum with its display

of British, Continental and American model railways in life-like miniature settings, can drive to Dobwalls for a trip on a full-size train in the Forest Railroad Park.

Here the age of steam out-west is recreated with two narrow gauge tracks plunging through tunnels into canyons and past waterfalls.

South of St Austell the rolling headlands are dotted with small, unspoilt coves and beaches where there is not even an ice-cream kiosk to mar the natural beauty. Energetic walkers can pick up the way-marked South West Coastal Footpath which runs for 515 miles from Poole in Dorset to Minehead in Somerset. For shorter strolls, the countryside is latticed with field and clifftop footpaths.

After a day's sunshine, exploring or golfing, take an evening drive through the high-banked lanes of the Roseland Peninsula to a country pub. Because this area is such a popular spot, many public houses have children's rooms as well as sizeable beer gardens. Stick to the coast road to see the tiny coves of Portloe, Portscatho and St Mawes where it is easy to imagine smugglers coming ashore with their contraband. Or strike off inland to the picture-postcard hamlets of Veryan, with its thatched-roofed roundhouses, and Philleigh.

Across St Austell Bay is Fowey, another tourist trap in mid-summer, but best enjoyed early in the morning or evening. The sign of the King of Prussia Inn commemorates one of Cornwall's most famous smugglers – John Car-ter who was a successful operator in these parts, but Henry VIII was more concerned with raids by the Spanish when he built St Catherine's Fort, one of several coastal strongholds.

Fowey stands at the mouth of a river bearing the same name which has a long estuary reach-ing almost to Lostwithiel. Along the whole of this stretch, fishing for salmon and sea trout is free although there is competition for water space from innumerable commercial craft and yachts in particular, as Fowey has become a popular sailing centre.

Whether you view the white mountains of St Austell with distaste or acceptance, they are as much part of Cornwall as the thrift-covered headlands and thick yellow ice-cream. Cer-tainly the Cornish are proud of this industry and the Wheal Martyn Museum records 150 years of mining history. Complete clay works of the last century have been restored with examples of the outdated machinery used and there is also a working pottery. This is a visit for dry days as Wheal Martyn is an open-air museum and it is liable to become a quagmire if rain is excessive.

**Angling**
River Fowey:
excellent sea trout
fishing Apr–May.
Free fishing from
Lostwithiel to sea.
Water Authority:
SWWA, 3–5
Barnfield Road,
Exeter
*Tel: (0392) 31666*

**Camping**
Carlyon Bay:
Bethesda
Camping site▶
*Tel: (072 681) 2735*
Sloping 200-pitch (50
caravans) grass site
Open Apr–Sep, must
book Jul–Aug
St Austell:
Trewhiddle Caravan
& Camping ▶▶▶
*Tel: (0726) 2659*
Secluded 125-pitch
site (25 caravans)
Open Jun–Sep, must
book Jul–Aug
Sticker: Glenleigh
Caravan Park▶
*Tel: (0726) 65633*
Level 40-pitch site
Open Apr–Oct, must
book Jul–Aug

**Riding**
St Austell: Porth Hall
Riding Centre,
Sticker
*Tel: (0726) 4103*

**Sailing**
Fowey: Fowey River
Sailing Centre, White
Walls, North Street
*Tel: (072 683) 2318*
Minimum 1 week
sailing courses

**General**
Fowey: Castle Dore:
Iron Age earthwork
2½m N of Fowey,
accessible all year. St
Catherine's Castle:
restored 16th-
century stronghold
Open all year daily
9–dusk
Probus: Trewithen
House: 18th-century
country house
Open Apr–Jul (Mon
& Tue pm only)
St Austell: Quillet
Homecrafts: soft
animals craft
workshop
Open usual hours,
but ring first
*Tel: (0726) 882454*
Wheal Martyn
Museum: open-air
site of china clay
works, water-
wheels, indoor
displays
Open Apr–Oct

# St Enodoc

St Enodoc, Rock, Wadebridge,
North Cornwall
*Tel: Trebetherick (020 886) 3216*

From Wadebridge follow B3314 (Port
Issac road) for 3 miles. Turn right to
Rock.
Two seaside courses: 6069yds: SSS69;
2002yds: SSS59
*Course designer:* James Braid

Visitors welcome with club introduction
for 18-hole course
*Professional* E W Goodman

Hotels: St Moritz ★★ Trebetherick
*Tel: (020 886) 2242*
(60rm)

St Enodoc ★★ Rock
*Tel: (020 886) 2311*
(16rm)

Roskarnon House ★★ Rock
*Tel: (020 886) 2329*
(16rm)

If the quality of the golf was not so good, it would be almost impossible to play the game at St Enodoc because of the marvellous distractions. This is a holiday course *par excellence* on which completely natural scenery competes with high golfing adventure and great fun on

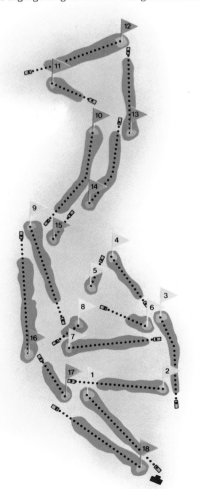

some of the best links-land in the country.

Situated behind the delightful hamlet of Rock on the north side of the Camel estuary facing Padstow, St Enodoc has a vista of fine golden beaches, waters flecked with the sails of scores of small boats and the flash of light from a water ski-ier's wake. From every tee is a glimpse of the sea – and as most golfers find to their cost, beauty is distracting at all times.

Golf started at St Enodoc in 1888 when undergraduates played around the area of the little church (then newly-unearthed from the sands) and the beaches of Daymer Bay. A year later a few holes were laid out in the dunes at Rock and the present club was founded around 1891. The club leased most of the land on which the links now stand in 1905 from a Dr Theophilus Hoskin who is now buried in St Enodoc graveyard. Since 1949 the land has been part of the Duchy of Cornwall estates. It is the legendary James Braid who set out the club's present 18 holes (there is also a nine-hole on the site).

It takes a man of courage to commit himself to the direction post across the rolling expanse of the first hole, which funnels down into a narrow valley between dunes, a testing second shot. It is only through this gap that the green can be reached with composure. In fact the first three holes shake a visitor's confidence as the player must be convinced that straight shots are possible – without them the score will already be in shreds quite a long time before reaching the short 4th.

A sight of the great 'Himalaya' sandhill at

the 6th and the only slightly less imposing mound on the 7th can strike terror in the heart. Both have to be cleared by the second shot. This is, however, the end of the dunes for a while. From the 8th a different world greets the player. Magic carpets of flowers, clusters of orchids, and an atmosphere of remoteness and peace prevails – that is if the occasionally ferocious seawinds are not on the blow. From the 10th one gets a glimpse of the famous little church of St Enodoc which, apart from its squat tower, disappeared from view for centuries, swamped by drifting sands. A religious site since Norman times the church was only unearthed and re-used in 1863. The 10th is a dogleg for which, with a little luck, the second shot might be conveniently sighted on the church porch.

It takes four holes to skirt round the church, a section of the links closed on Sundays at the request of Hoskin's widow until as recently as the early Thirties. The 12th tee is practically on the beach of Daymer Bay and is frequently covered by drifting sand. It is far too easy to stand here and dream, bewitched by the tang of the sea and Cornwall's own peculiar magic. Sir John Betjeman was captivated enough to play this section of the course in verse and eulogised his birdie on the 13th.

'The very turf rejoiced to see
The quite unprecedented three'

The player will in fact find the springy turf pleasant and on a good day the shot-making is simple enough – remember, though, it is the Atlantic out there and wind is very often the

streets run downhill to Padstow's harbour, still the village's centre of attraction after centuries as one of Cornwall's major trading ports. The quayside is always peppered with young boys and their grandfathers, with tins of worm bait and lines delving the murky waters of the harbour. It is from here that the more adventurous anglers set out to catch shark and porbeagle.

More appealing to many will be the delicate winged creatures at the Tropical Bird and Butterfly Gardens where a number of breeds from all over the world are successfully bred and reared. Visitors can walk among the tropical and sub-tropical foliage to watch both animals in free flight. The butterflies are livelier on sunny summer days.

Wadebridge is not only a river crossing. An unusual garden commemorates Queen Elizabeth II's coronation and the Cornish Motor Museum exhibits splendid vintage cars and veteran traction engines. In the days when these machines were the latest invention, most Cornish people lived poorly and simply. But grand mansions do exist, and Pencarrow House at Washaway is graced with marbled pillars and the Music Room has a rococo ceiling. Browsing among French and Oriental china and furniture and a gallery of 18th-century paintings will while away a wet afternoon, and if it is sunny there are thirty-five acres of woodland gardens with arrowed trails to explore.

There is greater freedom for walkers along the National Trust-owned coastline north of Polzeath to just short of Bude, with notable outcrops to view the Atlantic breaking against the rocks at The Rumps, Pentire Point and Tintagel Head. Delabole boasts a slate quarry which has been worked since Tudor times and claims it is the largest man-made hole in England. A museum and craft shop are open to the public during weekdays.

Those ghosties, ghoulies and long-legged beasties have found a fitting location. For things going bump in the night are guaranteed

**Angling**
River Allen: Camel tributary with fair game fishing
Daily (or weekly) tickets: A E Cave & Son, Polmorla Road, Wadebridge
*Tel: (020 881) 2591*
Water Authority: SWWA,
3–5 Barnfield Road, Exeter
*Tel: (0392) 31666*
River Camel: a principal game river with good access
Tickets: as River Allen
Water Authority: as River Allen

**Camping**
Padstow: Penjoly Caravan Park ▶▶
*Tel: (0841) 532289*
Level 25-pitch site (5 tents)
Open Easter–Sep, must book Jul–Aug
St Mabyn: Glenmorris Caravan & Camping Park ▶▶▶▶
*Tel: (020 884) 236*
Rural 150-pitch site
Open Apr–Oct, must book Jul–Aug
St Minver: St Minver House Holiday Estate ▶▶▶
*Tel: (020 886) 2305*
Flat 233-pitch site
Open May–mid-Sep, must book Jul–Aug

**Riding**
Camelford: Tall Tree

Stables, Davidstow
*Tel: (084 06) 249*

**Walking Trails**
Port Quin to Rock 7m (2½ hour) coastal walk with fine views along Camel estuary. Start from Port Quin, 3m W of Port Isacc

**General**
Bodmin: Military Museum: relics & items of The Duke of Cornwall's Light Infantry
Open Apr–Feb Mon–Fri
Pencarrow House: impressive Georgian mansion 3m NW of Bodmin
Open Easter–Sep (ex Mon & Sat)
*Tel: (020 884) 369*
Delabole: Delabole Slate Quarry & Museum: ancient 500ft-deep working quarry, 3m W of Camelford off B3314
Open Easter then May–Sep (ex Sat & Sun)
*Tel: (084 02) 2242*
Padstow: Tropical Bird & Butterfly Gardens: free-flying birds, rare plants
Open all year
*Tel: (0841) 532262*
Wadebridge: Hustyn Mill: design & craft centre near Wadebridge
Open most times
*Tel: (020 881) 2540*

governing factor. The last three holes require considerable power to your arm, the 16th being the longest hole of all at 482 yards for a par 5.

St Enodoc has been a major centre for Cornish and South Western Championships. The 1937 English Ladies Championship at St Enodoc was celebrated for two reasons. Wanda Morgan won the title for the second year running and the beautiful, somewhat mysterious, and completely unrated Miss Gladys Minoprio appeared on the competitive scene. Soundly beaten during the first round on which she had played every shot with one club, a cleek, she is remembered only as the first woman to wear slacks on a golf course.

Non-playing members of the family have equally breath-taking country to explore, literally. For just around the headland from Daymer Bay is the prime surfing beach of Polzeath. You do not have to be up to Malibu beach standard to enjoy the exhilarating experience of riding the Atlantic rollers – basic straight boards can be hired quite cheaply from a number of small shops that skirt the beach. For a leisurely swim, return to Daymer, perhaps via the springy turf of the cliff-top walk which avoids a gear-churning, congested coast road. Rockpools give hours of idle exploration at low tide and the sand dunes shelter picnickers from the fierce wind.

Across the Camel is the mediaeval village of Padstow, which can be reached romantically by a small ferry from Rock or by road via Wadebridge and the 15th-century thirteen-arch bridge that spans the river. Quaint old

at Boscastle, where the sea thunders through a narrow neck of rock to a small harbour. Here a museum of Witchcraft and Black Magic traces an awesome history of 'goings on' in the West Country, but for more harmless fun, see Tintagel with its convincing associations with the legendary King Arthur, or visit the beautiful Trebarwith Strand.

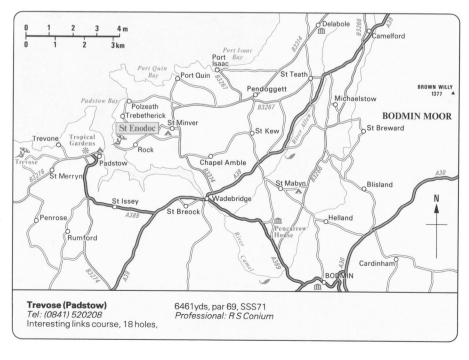

**Trevose (Padstow)**
*Tel: (0841) 520208*
Interesting links course, 18 holes,

6461yds, par 69, SSS71
*Professional: R S Conium*

# Royal North Devon and Saunton

Royal North Devon, Westward Ho!, North Devon
*Tel: Bideford (023 72) 3817*

Saunton, Braunton, North Devon
*Tel: Braunton (0271) 812436*

Royal North Devon

From Bideford take Northam road turning right at post office

Seaside course: 5960yds: SSS72
*Course designer:* Tom Morris

Visitors welcome
*Professional:* S Taggart

Saunton

From Barnstaple take B3231 to Braunton then bear left to club

Two seaside courses (one championship): 6675yds: SSS73; 6322yds: SSS71
*Course designers:* (Old) Herbert Fowler (New) Frank Pennink

Visitors welcome with letter of introduction from own club
*Professional:* J A MacGhee

Hotels: Durrant House ★★★ Bideford
*Tel: (023 72) 2361*
(58rm)

Yeoldon House ★★ Bideford
*Tel: (023 72) 4400*
(10rm)

Royal ★★ Bideford
*Tel: (023 72) 2005*
(34rm)

Tucked away on a remote section of the North Devon coast, and on opposite sides of the wide Taw estuary, are two of the most august seaside courses in British golfing history. Rivalling Bournemouth in the close proximity of these chances for fascinating golf are the Royal North Devon at the curiously named Westward Ho! and its northerly neighbour Saunton, laid across Braunton Burrows. Both are carved from dunes and pebble ridges that are the result of the exposure of the coast to the full force of the Atlantic as the weather comes in across Barnstaple Bay but, unless you want to indulge in an endless debate, that is where the similarity ends.

Set out on common land known as Northam or Appledore Burrows and still grazed by cattle and sheep in parts, the Royal North Devon is England's oldest seaside links. Played over by local residents since the 1850s (notable among them was the vicar of Northam, the Reverend I H Gossett) a club was formed here in 1864 on the original course laid down by Scotsman

Tom Morris. The club gained its 'Royal' title only three years later, when the Prince of Wales included it on his itinerary.

Rough lowland salt pasture and dunes protected from the sea by the high Pebble Ridge give the course, substantially remodelled to its present form in 1908, its distinctive flavour. While much of the land is level, there are some splendid valleys and ridges, the latter often being the site for a green. With so much sand around, it is no surprise that most of the holes are a commando course of bunkers. Most terrifying aspect of all is the giant sleepered bunker straddling the 4th, almost certainly the greatest hurdle in the country.

The course starts beguilingly enough with a tee-shot over the narrow extension of Goosey Pool that is tagged 'The Burn', and a canter on to a reasonably attainable par 5. By now the visitor will be uncomfortably aware of the fact that the course is nowhere near as flat as it looks from the clubhouse. The 3rd, on to a green ringed by the pock marks of bunkers, is made more interesting by skirting the seawater lake and then you face that shored-up sandhill of the 4th. You should carry over this from the tee if the day is right!

The way over this obstacle leads into the dunes of the bay shore, where a second more natural hazard reveals itself. There are two types of sea rushes at Westward Ho! – the smaller species is dismissively known locally as 'fog' and few players will escape a clump or two

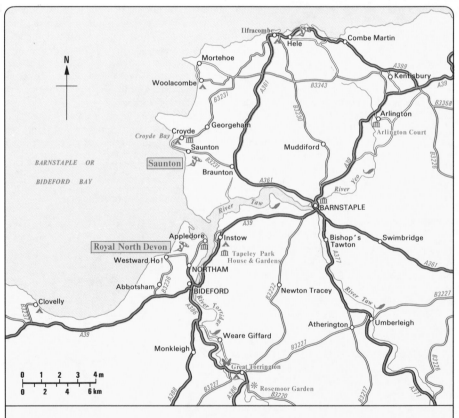

**Ilfracombe**
Tel: (0271) 62176
Clifftop course with fine views, 18 holes, 5823yds, par 69, SSS68
*Professional:* D Hoare

**Torrington**
Tel: (023 72) 2792
Hard-walking, scenic course, 9 holes, 4410yds, par 64, SSS63

*Picturesque Clovelly*

of them somewhere on the round. Far more intimidating are the Great Sea Rushes making the 10th and 11th holes look particularly impossible. If one was to pick a particular feature of Westward Ho!, the four short holes at five, eight, fourteen and sixteen are memorable. The 16th is the most exasperating of these, where any other than a pinpoint, accurate shot will see the ball tipped off the green plateau.

The route from here to the clubhouse is anything but smooth – waiting for all is that final trap of 'The Burn' (so easy to forget after a smooth passage of hole one) barring access to the 18th green.

About the Royal North Devon there is that faint whiff of similarity to St Andrews. The club is, after all, a cradle of English links golf and it is steeped in tradition. On the centenary, Christy O'Connor and Max Faulkner donned the garb of the founders, used a gutty ball and played a tremendously entertaining foursome with Peter Aliss and Brian Huggett. Only two years before, the club's greatest president, five-time Open winner J H Taylor had died aged ninety-two. A local man from Northam, Taylor caddied for the club's early celebrities such as Horace Hutchinson and learned the game by watching many of the greats at play.

Saunton, where perhaps the game spread from Westward Ho!, has its own foothold in golf history. It is indisputably one of the finest links in the country with the sea in view from

**SAUNTON GOLF COURSE**

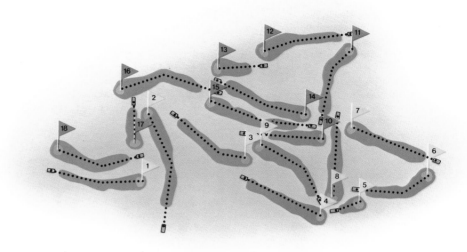

every tee. Had it been in a more accessible spot it would certainly have been high on the championship roster earlier in its development from the nine-holer first laid down in 1897 on flat lands adjacent to the infinitely more suitable scrub and dunes a mere shot away.

Sandhills and scrub make for great golfing country and Braunton Burrows, a 1000-acre duneland backing Saunton Sands is one of the largest plots of its kind in Britain. It is a paradise for bird-watchers and botanists, showing off the same wild profusion of flowers as St Enodoc further south on the coast.

In the early days, the members were quartered next door to the village post office and it was not until 1906 that a clubhouse was built to coincide with extension of the course to 18 holes on the lands closer to the sea. Between the wars the course was extensively remodelled by Herbert Fowler, the present clubhouse being built in 1929. A New Course was laid out by Fowler in 1935 but the intervention of the war and its use as a battle training ground lost the course to golf. It was not until 1952 that the land was returned to the Christie family and the Old Course was remodelled yet again by C K Cotton with new 1st, 2nd, 17th and 18th holes, its present length of a healthy 6675 yards and a standard scratch score of 72. Finally a new course, the West Course, was built in 1973 under the direction of J J F Pennink and the Old became the East Course.

Few opening holes are more severe than those on the East Course. Three of the first four are over 440 yards and all are hard-fought par 4s. There are only three short holes – the 5th, at 112 yards, being none the less demanding for its size. The 8th has a blind drive across dunes and the par 4 9th demands real concentration in seeking out the little valley that is the gateway to the green nestling in hills.

The hole people crow about at Saunton is the 16th – if you are in any fit shape to take it after the 485-yard par 5 of the 15th. You tee off blind over a hill guarding a considerably lower fairway before winding left over a deep bunker and on to a green ringed by dunes.

The West Course is partly on land that was used for the original New Course and while the terrain over the first few holes is very similar to

that of the Old, it wends its way into some of the higher dunes of the area. Holes of note on this round are the 426-yard 7th which is marked by a ditch that has to be crossed twice from an elevated tee shot and second shot to a green, raised but surrounded by dunes, and the 189-yard par 3 16th. Short it might be, but the tee is quite lofty, the green is heavily-bunkered and visitors may also tangle with the devious ditch to the right.

The reputation of these courses is matched only by the claims of Woolacombe for another sport. Surfing has been enjoyed here since the early days of the sport in Britain as the conditions are ideal. Two miles of sandy beach facing due west into the Atlantic where even on a calm day the rollers can reach up to six-foot high. Flags indicate the safest surfing and swimming areas and surf boards can be hired from the beach. For a less envigorating swim, Combe Martin, Mortehoe and the shell-studded strand of Barricane Beach are within a few miles' drive.

To the south of these courses, west of Clovelly, lies an area of incredible natural beauty. It is known as Hartland. The National Trust owns a good deal of this wild, dramatic county. Drive to Hartland Quay and walk over steep clifftops festooned with colourful plants to view the intriguing waterfall which tumbles on to rocks and smooth, golden sand far below. There is a good chance that there will only be seagulls to keep you company.

People have been flocking to Ilfracombe since Victoria's reign and it is still the largest seaside resort in North Devon, with good beaches, summer attractions – and crowds. Among places to visit are Chambercombe Manor, one of the oldest inhabited houses in England which boasts a haunted room, and Hele Mill which was built in 1525. It has been lovingly restored and now produces wholemeal flour. On a sunny day you can board a steamer and cruise along the coast and across the Bristol Channel. The boats link Ilfracombe with Cardiff, Bristol, Swansea and Lundy Island.

Lundy is a granite outcrop inhabited by ponies, sika deer, wild and nimble goats and the rare trap-door spider. Humans only visit, either to stalk and study colonies of seabirds

**Angling**
River Taw: good game & coarse fishing with some chances for visitors. Free fishing from Week (4m S of Barnstaple) to sea Water Authority: SWWA, 3–5 Barnfield Road, Exeter *Tel: (0392) 31666* River Yeo: Taw tributary offering trout & sea trout Daily tickets (Mon–Fri only): The Rod Room, 93 Boutport Street, Barnstaple *Tel: (0271) 5360* Water Authority: as River Taw

**Camping**
Croyde Bay: Ruda Holiday Park▶▶▶ *Tel: (0271) 890671* Gently-rolling 400-pitch site Open Easter–Oct, must book Jul–Aug Ilfracombe: Big Meadow Camping Site▶ *Tel: (0271) 62282* 150-pitch site near sea Open May–Oct no bookings Woolacombe: Woolacombe Bay Caravan Park▶ *Tel: (027 187) 221* Sloping 230-pitch site (50 caravans) Open mid-May – mid-Oct, must book

**Walking Trails**
Cowley Cleave Nature Trail: ⅓m (½hour) signposted woodland walk. Take turning to Parracombe 8m E of Ilfracombe off A399

**General**
Arlington: Arlington Court: 1822 mansion in wooded estate – pewter, model ships & seashell collections. Open Apr–Oct daily 11–6 Barnstaple: The North Devon Athenaeum: museum with geological, fossil & butterfly collections Open all year (ex Sat pm & Sun) *Tel: (0271) 2174* Croyde: Croyde Gem, Rock & Shell Museum: unique craft museum & workshop Open Mar–Oct daily (winter times restricted) *Tel: (0271) 890407* Ilfracombe: Hele Mill: 16th-century working flour mill Open Easter–Sep (ex Sat) *Tel: (0271) 63162* Lundy Island: tiny Bristol Channel island, breeding place of many rare birds. Steamer service from Ilfracombe Quay May–Sep (no cars) *Tel: (0271) 62687*

and puffins, or to scale the 400-foot Granite Slide which is recognised by climbers as one of the finest sea-cliff ascents in Britain.

There are less exacting hills to climb at Combe Martin, where spoil tips from the old silver mines contain large lumps of crystalline lead and silver ores and fool's gold (iron pyrites). The hilltops are reached by the old mule and pack horse trails, narrow-walled gulleys set with stone steps that were built by the miners. Combe Martin itself is a straggling long village with a harbour and the Pack of Cards Inn, constructed like a house of cards, with each storey smaller than the one below. It is said to have been built by a man who made a fortune at gambling.

The curiously named village of Westward Ho! was virtually unknown until it was named after the Kingsley novel in 1855. Its other literary connection is with Kipling, for it is here that the tales of schoolboy adventures *Stalky & Co* were based. R D Blackmore chose North Molton as the setting for part of *Lorna Doone*, and John Gay (who wrote *The Beggar's Opera*) was educated at the local Barnstaple grammar school.

Bideford, at the mouth of the River Torridge, used to be North Devon's principal port, handling cargoes of American tobacco. A notable bridge which spans the river is 677-feet long and has twenty-four arches – some of it is 15th-century. Just north of the town is the small, picturesque fishing village of Appledore. Small Georgian houses line cobbled streets which lead down to a sandy beach and a

small quay. The village is the home of the North Devon Maritime Museum where models in authentic settings, photographs and paintings illustrate the region's long and vivid maritime history.

Walkers are spoilt by miles of National Trust headland – Morte Point, Baggy Point and Woolacombe Warren. Along the northern side of the Taw estuary are the sandy dunelands of Braunton Burrows which support rare botanical species and uncommon seabirds. Trails through the wasteland are way-marked and should be strictly followed, as much of this land is still used as a military training ground. For intensive use of leg muscles, drive to the car park above Clovelly and walk down to the quayside. It is a 400-foot descent down cobbled streets and often slippery stone slabs worn smooth by the feet of thousands of visitors each year. It is not only the challenge of reaching the bottom (and getting back) which attracts them. Clovelly is almost unbelievably quaint with colour-washed cottages festooned with flowering window boxes.

More than fifty years ago Bernard Darwin, the doyen of golf writers, put the following on record: 'One thing is certain about Saunton, that there never was a spot in the whole world more obviously intended for a golf course. The splendour of its hills and valleys must be seen to be believed.' It is a eulogy that can equally be applied to the Royal North Devon and if you are lucky enough to stay close to this bewitching twosome for a holiday you will not fail to be captivated.

**ROYAL NORTH DEVON GOLF COURSE**

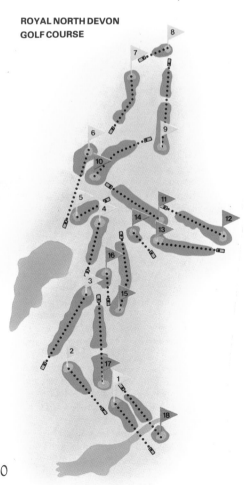

**Angling**
Bideford: good shore fishing at Appledore & Bideford Quay for bass, cod, flounder, plaice. Plus gurnard, tope & turbot by boat
Tackle shop: B & K Angling, The Quay, Bideford
*Tel: (023 72) 4613*
River Taw: good game & coarse fishing with some chances for visitors
Free fishing from Week (4m S of Barnstaple) to sea
Water Authority: SWWA, 3–5 Barnfield Road, Exeter
*Tel: (0392) 31666*
River Torridge: fine trout & salmon towards estuary
Daily tickets (from riparian owner): C R Rowe, The Holt, Appledore
*Tel: (023 72) 3126*
Water Authority: as River Taw

**Camping**
Clovelly:
Steart Farm ▶▶▶
*Tel: (023 73) 239*
Undulating 60-pitch site, 5m E of Clovelly
Open Easter–Oct, no bookings
Gt Torrington:
Greenways Valley
Holiday Park ▶▶
*Tel: (080 52) 2153*
Level 10-pitch site

(no tents). Open mid-May–Oct, no booking
Instow: Lagoon View Caravan Park ▶
*Tel: (0271) 860423*
Slightly sloping 28-pitch site (no tents)
Open Easter–Sep, must book Aug

**General**
Appledore: N Devon Maritime Museum: naval paintings, craft & models
Open Easter–Sep daily 2.30–5.30
Barnstaple:
Marwood Hill: 10 acres of rare trees, shrubs & gardens
Open all year
*Tel: (0271) 2528*
Gt Torrington:
Rosemoor Garden: modern garden with many shrubs & trees
Open Apr–Oct daily
Instow: Tapeley Park House & Gardens: Italianate garden, woodland walks, putting green
Open Easter–Oct 10–6 (ex Mon)
*Tel: (0271) 860528*
Shebbear: Alscott Farm Agricultural Museum: fascinating collection of vintage farm implements plus scale model exhibits, 9m S of Gt Torrington off A388
Open Easter–Sep daily
*Tel: (040 928) 206*

# Manor House Hotel

Manor House Hotel

Moretonhampstead, Devon
*Tel: Moretonhampstead (064 74) 355*
*Telex: 42794*

2½ miles south west of Moretonhampstead on B3212

Parkland and moorland course: 6016yds; SSS69
*Course designers:* J F Abercromby/Frank Hole

Visitors welcome except at first tee before 10am April–November
*Professional:* A Macdonald

Hotels: Manor House Hotel ★★★★ 🏌 (66rm)
Bay Tree Motel ★ Crockernwell
*Tel: Drewsteignton (064 721) 267* (8rm)
Blenheim Hotel ★★ Brimley Road, Bovey Tracey
*Tel: (0626) 832422* (9rm)

Sited on the north east edge of the Dartmoor National Park is the quiet old market village of Moretonhampstead. A delightful heart of Devon touring centre, it is an ideal spot from which to explore the moors and the beautiful wooded valley of the Teign or to set out to cast a fly over the trout-filled rivers flowing off land that is truly Britain's last remaining wilderness. Increasingly, Moretonhampstead's name is being linked with first class golf, since the course on the Manor House Hotel's ground some two and a half miles west of the village was developed to its full potential.

It is not unusual these days to find a hotel possessing its own golf course, but this one is a jewel, with the scenery to match. Set some 700-feet up on the lower slopes of Dartmoor, this glorious course is no playground for the gentle forays of guests. Rather it is a demanding test of a player's repertoire and ingenuity. Many keen golfers will be familiar with the opening holes of the Manor House as they were the location for Peter Alliss's television series of instruction. These are the beautiful holes that wind and flirt with the fast-flowing trout waters of the River Bovey. In fact the best of

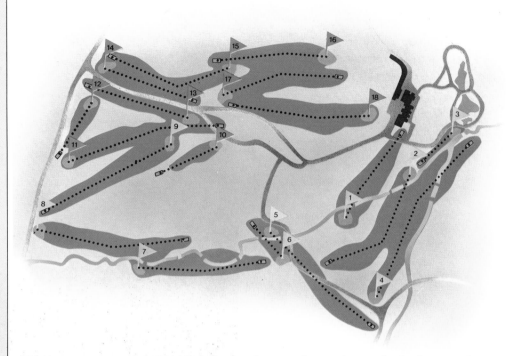

**Angling**
River Teign: good
game river, at its best
in Spring.
Daily tickets (in
advance): J Bowden
& Son, The Square,
Chagford
*Tel: (064 73) 3271*
Water Authority:
SWWA, 3–5
Barnfield Road,
Exeter
*Tel: (0392) 31666*

**Camping**
Chudleigh Knighton:
Ford Farm▶
*Tel: (0626) 853253*
Small 48-pitch site
(18 caravans)
Open Mar–Oct must
book for caravans
Moretonhampstead:
Clifford Bridge
Caravan Park▶▶▶
*Tel: (064 724) 226*
Grassy 20-pitch site
(no tents) 3m NE of
Moretonhampstead
off B3212
Open mid-Mar–Oct,
must book Jul–Aug

**Riding**
Newton Abbot:
Pinchaford Riding
Centre (J R Shelton),
Haytor
*Tel: (036 46) 251*

**Walking Trails**
Yarner Wood
National Nature
Reserve: marked trail
through trees, rich in
birds. Permit at lodge
4m NW of Bovey
Tracey off B3344

**General**
Ashburton:
Ashburton Museum:
local antiquities,
geology & weaponry.
Open May–Sep (Tue,
Thu, Fri & Sat
afternoons)
*Tel: (0364) 52298*
Drewsteignton:
Castle Drogo:
modern granite
castle off A382
Open Apr–Oct 11–6
Exeter: Custom
House: 17th-century
brick building.
Open all year
*Tel: (0392) 74021*
Underground
Passages: ancient
city aqueducts
Open all year 2–4.30
(ex Sun & Mon)
*Tel: (0392) 56724*
Newton Abbot: New
Devon Pottery:
pottery & leather
workshops.
Open Easter–Oct
daily (ex Sat & Sun)
*Tel: (0626) 4262*

players will be relieved to keep the ball above water while negotiating the first eight holes. Woven around the many twists and turns of the river, the fairways have been designed through a green, tree-lined valley abounding in rhododendrons and ferns.

At the 1st hole the river intrudes straight away, as it is possible to carry over it with a good tee shot – first-timers may make it on a more timorous second. At Water's Meet, the short 3rd hole (160-yard), the green is set in a cluster of rhododendrons and bordered by the river to the right – all too easy to plunge the ball in. There is very little relief on the 530-yard 4th hole which follows a stone boundary wall, now doubling as a trap for hookers. The 6th does offer some chances to even up your score card with a par 3 before you are hurled into the maelstrom of the aptly named Styx. This is the last dangerous intrusion of the river which must be avoided at all costs to the right and not forgotten as it meanders its way into the line to the green.

You leave the river behind after the 8th and begin the climb to the top of the hotel grounds. From the 9th tee, the moorland view opens up and the golf becomes distinctly different. There are new problems to overcome but you at least get a chance to flex your muscles. Some good strokes are needed for the 9th, the 11th and the short 12th.

An avenue of trees borders the fairway of the 14th and you are still climbing to the heights of Manor Tor which hold the delights of the 16th and 17th holes. Last hurdle before safely reaching the hotel's front door is a blind second shot to be taken on the final hole before you can claim your Devonshire cream tea.

The hotel and the course have an interesting history. Manor House is a member of the British Transport Hotels group, like its larger cousins Gleneagles and Turnberry, and the land is an inheritance from the Great Western Railway. Originally designed by J F Abercromby, the course was opened in 1930, but indifferent management and its less-than-challenging 5600-yard length led to its slow decline during the following years. Moreton-hampstead's revival was under the direction of Frank Hole. He drew on the original design and added length to take every advantage of the superb natural hazards. Over the now 6260-yard course, the record of 66 has been held for many years by Norman Sutton of Exeter, who is now retired after a notable tournament career.

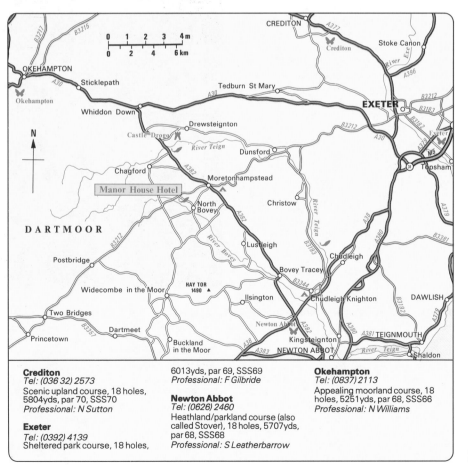

**Crediton**
*Tel: (036 32) 2573*
Scenic upland course, 18 holes,
5804yds, par 70, SSS70
*Professional: N Sutton*

**Exeter**
*Tel: (0392) 4139*
Sheltered park course, 18 holes,
6013yds, par 69, SSS69
*Professional: F Gilbride*

**Newton Abbot**
*Tel: (0626) 2460*
Heathland/parkland course (also
called Stover), 18 holes, 5707yds,
par 68, SSS68
*Professional: S Leatherbarrow*

**Okehampton**
*Tel: (0837) 2113*
Appealing moorland course, 18
holes, 5251yds, par 68, SSS66
*Professional: N Williams*

# Queen's Park and Parkstone

Queen's Park, West Drive,
Bournemouth, Dorset
*Tel: Bournemouth (0202) 36198*

Parkstone, Poole, Dorset
*Tel: Canford Cliffs (0202) 708025*

Queen's Park

3 miles north of Bournemouth town
centre adjacent to B3347

Parkland and seaside course: 6505yds:
SSS72
*Course designer:* J H Taylor

Visitors welcome
*Professional:* J Sharkey

Parkstone

Heathland course: 6250yds: SSS70
*Course designer:* W Park

Visitors welcome after 9.30am. No play
to start between 1–2pm
*Professional:* K Hockey

Hotels: wide selection in Bournemouth
and Poole

Bournemouth, perhaps alone among the stately resort towns of the South Coast so beloved of the Victorians, has managed to retain much of its sea-front splendour and reputation for health-giving airs. It is a town of gardens and clusters of pine woods where 100-foot cliffs rise above splendid safe beaches and, if you believe the brochures, the climate is mild and rough weather is just 'bracing and invigorating'. Small surprise then, that Bournemouth has long been a centre for the kind of sports that have an appeal to its fashionable clientele. County cricket and tennis tournaments are regular crowd pullers, but it is the tremendous opportunities for golf in the area of this resort that take some beating.

Within a few miles are the fabulous 6505-yard Queen's Park municipal course and 6250-yard Parkstone. Bournemouth has a second municipal course at Meyrick Park and the final jewel is Broadstone at nearby Poole.

Queen's Park and Parkstone share the fact that they are both carved from the natural pine and heather-clad heath of the area and both provide, for differing reasons, stimulating golf. Queen's Park in particular is regarded as one of the most stretching of the area with many a fabled professional coming to grief on its accuracy-demanding, tree-lined fairways.

Queen's Park has been the scene of many top international tournaments including the Penfold, the Martini and, in 1980, the Carlsberg Ladies' Championship. It is a course that lulls golfers into a false sense of well-being with its comparatively easy par 4 and par 3 start. Stay awake, however, as the going gets considerably tougher with two par 5s in the next four holes. Hole four, for instance, is a long dogleg of very fast-running fairway, there is the brief respite of the very short 5th and then comes the 483-yard 6th. Both this hole and the 445-yard 8th can become nightmares in the prevailing south-westerly wind. A double dogleg may bring you within an ace of the closely guarded 10th green and you will excel to make the par 5.

Most of the praise of Queen's Park is centred on hole thirteen, which is appropriately enough, reckoned to be among the toughest holes in the south of England. The golfer first has to thread the ball down an avenue of trees avoiding a hook at all cost, while knowing that to stray the other way plunges the ball into the gaping jaws of one of a series of bunkers. The 15th is longer but after this monster of a hole, Queen's Park holds few surprises during the predominantly short holes that remain.

Like most of the courses in this selection, Queen's Park has had its historic moments. While it was being readied for opening in 1905 James Braid played the then equally famous

*Parkstone*

**QUEEN'S PARK GOLF COURSE**

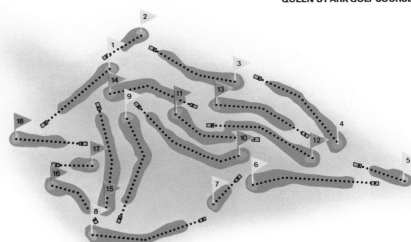

so'. Queen's Park was further redesigned in 1965 to take in a new clubhouse and better access for players' cars.

Parkstone was opened in 1910 and was also redesigned by James Braid in 1927 when the land was purchased from Lord Wimborne. The original design was by that pioneer of modern course-building, Willie Park.

Other Parkstone claims to fame are its association with the golfing Whitcombe brothers (Reg, the youngest, was the professional there) and the Alliss brothers Peter and Alec became joint professionals in 1957. Peter Alliss, now a television celebrity, represented Britain many times in Ryder Cup contests and following his performance in 1965, when he took five out of six matches, he was made an honorary member of Parkstone.

It is a scenic course set like an emerald in an area of luxury homes, almost half-way between Bournemouth and Poole. From the course golfers have views over Poole harbour. Brownsea Island rears in the middle ground, capped

by its castle and in the far distance is the mass of the Purbeck Hills. The dry, sandy heath on which it is built makes the playing dry underfoot and although the course ascends no great heights, there is the draw of the tremendous variety of trees and shrubs (including big banks of rhododendrons) that dot the grounds.

As at Queen's Park there is an easy run-up to the more serious aspects of the Parkstone course – even the 3rd, 490 yards at par 5, raises few problems, with its lakeside bounds and bunker trap to the left of the green. The challenge has to be taken up at the 4th which rates a par 4 at only 275 yards, with its narrow entrance to the green through a bunkered gate. The gauntlet is truly thrown down at the 6th with its long dogleg around trees uphill to a view of the green.

Players now have to cross the busy Lilliput Road where once there was a drive over the traffic to hole seven. Running uphill again on three plateaux, the major feature of this stiff par 3 is a massive bunker across the fairway.

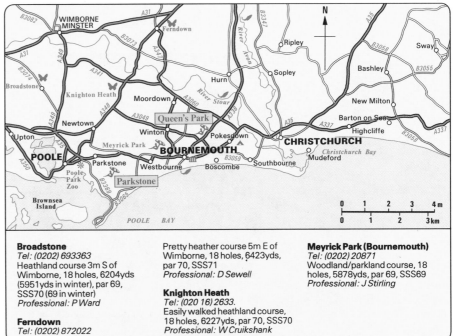

professional Harry Varden and scored 74, Varden coming home with an extra stroke on his card. Braid later became consultant to the council for the 1935 reconstruction of the course. In these days of equal opportunity it is interesting to recall that this was the year Bournemouth passed the course rule allowing ladies to play Queen's Park only on certain days. This was 'on the express condition that they will at all times, and under all circumstances, allow gentlemen players to pass them on the course without being requested to do

**Broadstone**
*Tel: (0202) 693363*
Heathland course 3m S of Wimborne, 18 holes, 6204yds (5951yds in winter), par 69, SSS70 (69 in winter)
*Professional: P Ward*

**Ferndown**
*Tel: (0202) 872022*

Pretty heather course 5m E of Wimborne, 18 holes, 6423yds, par 70, SSS71
*Professional: D Sewell*

**Knighton Heath**
*Tel: (020 16) 2633.*
Easily walked heathland course, 18 holes, 6227yds, par 70, SSS70
*Professional: W Cruikshank*

**Meyrick Park (Bournemouth)**
*Tel: (0202) 20871*
Woodland/parkland course, 18 holes, 5878yds, par 69, SSS69
*Professional: J Stirling*

Bunkers also beset the right of the green. If you reckon to have a lengthy tee-shot on the right day, it is tempting to aim over the small copse of silver birches to the right of the fairway at hole eight – wiser players will take the dogleg down the fairway. It is from this high tee that the vista from Parkstone opens up, to be viewed again from the 13th.

This is another clever left-hand dogleg, deservedly par 4 over its 360 yards. The tee is high and it may be entirely reasonable to carry over the bunker confronting your second shot – but do not make the mistake of misjudging the elevation of the green!

The remaining hurdle is the 17th which has right and left hand greens – the one in use will be indicated at the tee. Do not be tempted, if you have knowledge of one, to play it as you would the other. Old Man's Alley is the safe way down the fairway to the right hand hole but you will have to place the second shot much more carefully to get an opening on to the left hand green. To finish the round, the short 18th offers quite a drop to the front and left of the green, which will rob you of the final par 3 if you do not take sufficient care.

You could not leave this area without at least a look at Broadstone, different again from Queen's Park and Parkstone but also once part of Lord Wimborne's estate. Carved from the same heath as Parkstone, it is set at a railway junction and three bridges are to be walked on its 6204-yard round of springy turf among heather and gorse. Wickedest hole of all is the infamous 17th, featuring a deep gully with a 'safe' landing on an intervening plateau of gorse and finally an elevated green – all on a straight drive for par 4!

For many people these excellent courses are only a part of the sporting action. National tennis tournaments are held at Bournemouth's hardcourts, there are league football and county cricket matches played at Dean Park. Just about every participator sport is covered from athletics, squash and ice-skating to swimming, bowls and draughts. The area is an angler's paradise, too, with a choice of fishing.

The Solent teems with flatfish and a few miles away at Christchurch the Stour and Avon are accessible to visiting game and coarse fishermen. Deeper waters for catches of bass, cod and mackerel can be reached by hiring a boat from Mudeford or Christchurch.

There are opportunities for other forays by boat at several places along the coast. A pleasure trip through Studland Bay to Swanage passes the Old Harry Rocks or for a look round Poole harbour, board a vessel at Bournemouth Pier. From Poole Quay you can reach the National Trust island of Brownsea. Now a peaceful nature reserve with two lakes and a mile of bathing beach, it was the spot chosen by Lord Baden-Powell in 1907 for his first scout camp.

With an estimated one and a quarter million visitors each year, Bournemouth is geared to tourists in summer, and many locals have children's rooms and sheltered beer gardens. Cosmopolitan restaurants, ice-cream parlours and fish bars are informal. For evening entertainment, again there is an enormous choice. Concerts and plays (the town has its own Symphony Orchestra which has an international reputation) or variety shows with top celebrities are some examples. There are also seven cinemas, five casinos, nightclubs and discotheques.

Many day-time entertainments are exclusively for children. An Aqua Show, held annually between June and September at the Pier Approach Baths, alters only slightly from year to year. Proven ingredients are water ballet, comedy diving and performing sealions. A Punch and Judy man plays to a packed audience every day on the sands near the Pier, and during the Children's Festival, many of the clown and magic acts on the Promenade are free of charge.

For rainy days there are the treasures of the Russell-Coates Art Gallery and Museum to see. Many of them are Victorian or Oriental and there is a fascinating collection of Henry Irving's theatrical souvenirs. Rothesay Museum finds room for 350 typewriters in the world's only self-contained collection (the first commercial machine there is dated 1873). A marine room is devoted to relics from Sir Cloudesley Shovell's flagship HMS *Association* which sank in 1707.

On bright days, one of the best ways of seeing Bournemouth's parks, gardens and Victorian buildings is from the open top of a Yellow Sunshine bus. There are still more places to enjoy within a few miles' drive by car. To the west is the Isle of Purbeck dominated by the ruins of the Norman castle at Corfe, and famous for its stone which is worked by hand. Blocks of it were used in Westminster Abbey and several cathedrals.

Eastwards are the ancient hunting grounds of the New Forest, a mixture of heathery moors, dells and woodland, much of it cultivated with plantations. Wild ponies and cattle roam the glades and the temperate climate, country pubs and picnic spots attract hordes of country-lovers each year. The traditional way of seeing the Forest is by horseback, and there are plenty of riding stables throughout the area. The lazy way is by car, but perhaps the most rewarding is by walking. The Forestry Commission publishes booklets on several forest walks and nature trails.

Wherever golf comes on the list of holiday priorities, nobody left behind could complain of being in a desert with nothing to do. Seeing everything of interest is impossible – which should ensure a return visit.

### Angling

River Avon: top class trout & course fishing, but chances limited
Daily tickets: The Bailiff, Avon Buildings, Christchurch
Water Authority: WWA, Techno House, Redcliff Way, Bristol
*Tel: (0272) 25462/25491*
Bournemouth: shore fishing for bass, flounder, mullet, sole. Plus mackerel, shark, ray & turbot by boat
Tackle shop: Nimrod Sports, 9 Castle Parade, Ilford, Bournemouth
*Tel: (020 15) 78224*
River Stour: very good coarse fishing in lower reaches
Daily tickets: Taylor's Tackle, 258 Barrack Road, Christchurch
*Tel: (0202) 484518*
Water Authority: as River Avon

### Camping

Bournemouth: Cara Caravan Park ►►►
*Tel: (0202) 482121*
Scenic 40-pitch site (no tents)
Open all year, must book Jul–Aug
Chesildene Touring Caravan Park ►►►
*Tel: (0202) 513238*
Grassy 70-pitch site (no tents)
Open Apr–Oct, must book Jul–Aug

### Riding

Christchurch: Ashtree Riding School (A R Cook), Ashtree House, Purewell
*Tel: (0202) 482642*

### General

Bournemouth: Big Four Railway Museum: including large loco nameplate collection & working model railway
Open all year daily (Wed & Sat only in winter)
*Tel: (0202) 27995*
British Typewriter Museum: unique collection of over 300 typewriters
Open all year (ex Sun)
*Tel: (0202) 21009*
Compton Acres Gardens: 15 acres of fine rock & water gardens
Open Apr–Oct daily
*Tel: (0202) 708036*
Christchurch: Tucktonia: fascinating scaled miniatures of British buildings, plus leisure complex
Open Mar–Oct from 10
*Tel: (0202) 485100/482710*
Poole: Poole Park Zoo: small pleasant zoo
Open all year
*Tel: (0202) 745296*
Poole Pottery: noted craft workshop
Open all year
*Tel: (020 13) 2866*

**PARKSTONE GOLF COURSE**

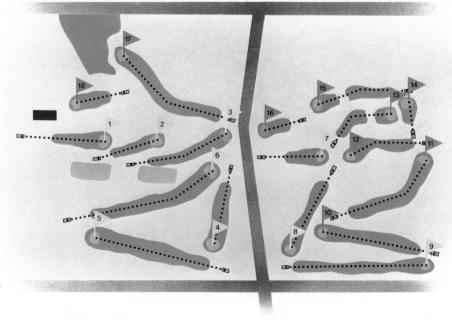

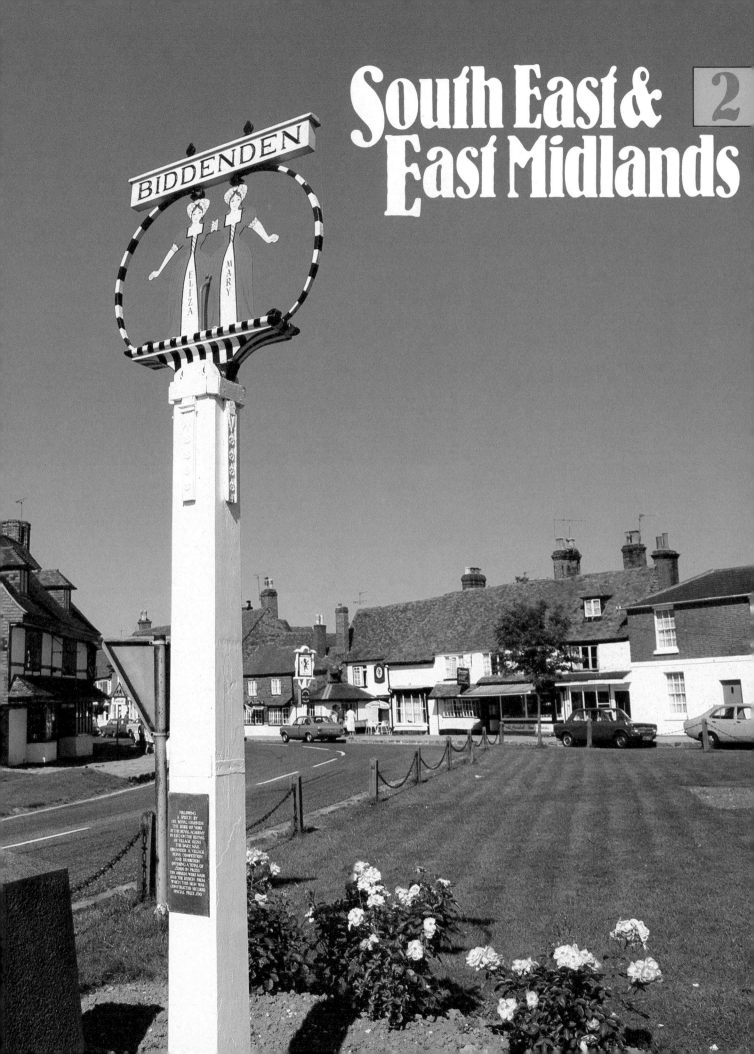

# West Sussex

Pulborough, West Sussex
*Tel: Pulborough (079 82) 2563*

On A283 mid-way between Pulborough and Storrington

Attractive heathland course: 6131yds, SSS70

Visitors welcome with club introduction except weekends or Bank Holidays
*Professional:* G Gledhill

Hotels: Abingworth Hall★★ Thakeham
*Tel: West Chiltington (079 83) 2257*
(14 rm)

Roundabout★★ West Chiltington
*Tel: West Chiltington (079 83) 3123*
(18 rm)

Swan★★ Fittleworth
*Tel: Fittleworth (079 882) 429*

That Pulborough should be the home of the West Sussex Golf Club is due to the remarkable vision of one man. It was Commander George Hillyard who realised in the Twenties that nestling under the South Downs, near to his home, was a piece of land similar in its character to outcrops of sandy heath which have produced great golf courses such as Woodhall Spa. Deep in a morass of Wealden clay was this fleck of heather-clad land which to Hillyard's eye spelt *golf*. He engaged Major Cecil Hutchison and Sir Guy Campbell to lay out the course. Barely had the ground settled into play after its 1930 opening, when Bernard Darwin was moved to write: 'The course is in fact a small sandy jewel in a setting of clay. There is enough of this precious ground to make one more admirable golf course, and there is no more.' As if more encouragement were needed to play here, noted golf architect, Tom Simpson, rates Pulborough among his top four heath courses in Britain.

Pulborough is a tiny town on the A29, the Roman road, Stane Street. The club is off the A283, halfway between Pulborough and Storrington. The area has good access from a large slice of the south coast and southern counties, which makes it a very popular society venue and one for which droves of touring golfers head. Give the secretary at least a day's notice of your intention to visit and you should be in luck. However, there are no occasional green fees on days booked by societies and at weekends. Pulborough's modest length of 6131 yards and club policy have kept the big golfing occasions away, to the benefit of visitors and members alike. It is a course that is none the less a searching test of golf for which the average player would be very happy to return a par of 67.

Fine white sand, contrasting with the deeper hues of heather and conifer and reflected in that prettiest of trees, the silver birch, are first visual impressions gained of Pulborough.

Heather encroaches on to the lines of the fairways at many holes, placing a premium on the straight drive. Unusually, there are no par 5s from Pulborough's medal tees (the 1st is used as a par 5 only in open competitions) so length is not the prime requisite. Accuracy is amply rewarded, and the short holes can be particularly challenging in this respect. For those who

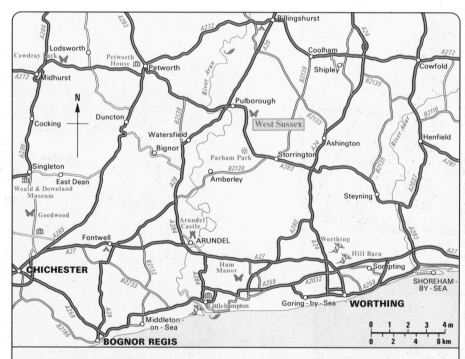

**Cowdray Park (Midhurst)**
Tel: (073 081) 3599
Parkland course with some hard walking, 18 holes, 6204yds, par 70, SSS70
*Professional: J Thomson*

**Goodwood**
Tel: (0243) 527491
Hilly course with fine views, 18 holes, 6004yds, par 69, SSS69

**Ham Manor**
Tel: (090 62) 3288
Interesting parkland course 2m E of Littlehampton off A259, 18 holes, 6216yds, par 70, SSS70
*Professional: P Marr*

**Hill Barn (Worthing)**
Tel: (0903) 37301
Easily walked downland course, 18 holes, 6083yds, par 70, SSS70

**Littlehampton**
Tel: (090 64) 7170
Pleasant seaside course, 18 holes, 6104yds, par 70, SSS69
*Professional: W Mackie*

**Worthing**
Tel: (0903) 60801
Two courses, both requiring accuracy, 18 holes, 6276yds (5084), par 70 (66), SSS70 (64)

do fall foul of the fine, brilliant sand, the wedge will be your best friend. Then there is the quality of Pulborough's turf. The velvety texture of the greens allow the errant putter absolutely no excuses.

Pulborough's 1st is typical of the lush fairways that permit the masterful driver to get up to the green in two – indeed that is one key to this course. There are several holes where, to stay abreast of the card, considerable length from the tee shot is a must.

In any event, length is not everything. Take the 4th, for example. It is a dogleg that should classically be taken in a drive and a short iron but anything less than absolute control will take you into closer proximity to the heather than you would care. From the 5th, you are into three fine short holes in four leaving only two for the home leg.

It is the 6th that forms, in most players' opinions, the real test. From an elevated tee you play over a valley which seems entirely filled, with little seasonal variation, by a marsh falling only sixty yards or so short of the green. Play short on your drive and it can mean one or two lost balls – but the sneaky way to a par 3 is to utilise a small patch of firm fairway to the right, getting up to the green through guard bunkers with an able second.

If your morale is still up to it, the 7th is one of Pulborough's driving holes on which the tee-shot has to carry a good proportion of its 442 yards. That is over a considerable ridge, the lip of which forms the upper limit of a cavernous bunker. The left of the green is also well-guarded.

A valley is the fearsome feature on the short 8th and presents the last real problem of the outward leg.

Returning home, the 10th begins in fine

style, with a long swing round to the left demanding considerable care and this is a softener for the 448-yard par 4 of the 11th. If ever there was a hole that seemed to play half the length again, this is it. A plateau green demands an extra club for the second shot and anything short makes it virtually impossible to get down on par.

Pulborough's remaining holes are a delightful journey. The 15th is a pretty par 3, played with a little pitch over a pond to gain most of the 132 yards – over-confidence might suggest a half shot and you will be one ball down. A deep gulley comes into play on the 16th. While it is true that Pulborough's architects could have found few more suited pieces of ground for golf in their long careers, they have drawn from it a course of real splendour that sees the county's professionals and amateurs returning year after year for their championships.

Most holidaying and touring families will base themselves on the coast which is only fifteen miles from Pulborough. Worthing, Littlehampton, Bognor Regis and Chichester are all within a comfortable half hour's drive of the course. These are the South Coast's more stately resorts, with something of a faded gentility. However if sun and sand make the ingredients of family holiday bliss, there is plenty of that. All four locations also have good sailing

facilities. Littlehampton in particular is a good spot for the sea angler (bass, cod, mullet and plaice may be taken from the quays and beaches and some boats may be hired in the harbour) and for fishing in the River Arun. The Arun flows off the downs through the Norman stronghold of Arundel, where the castle is open for most of the season.

Closer to Pulborough, walkers will find the heady views from the tops of the Downs a strong pull. Sections of the way-marked South Downs way can be joined at the car park on Chantry Hill near Storrington for a footpath circuit over Wepham Down and the slopes of Harrow Hill. There are more gentle walks on the nature trails of Fairmile Bottom near Madehurst and in Kingley Vale nature reserve near West Stoke.

If you are an outdoor type, there are some excellent campsites in the area, including one in the racecourse of Goodwood three miles north east of Chichester.

Journey anywhere in this corner of Sussex and the skyline is dominated by the Downs. An unusual museum, depicting the life in early settlements of this area, is the Weald and Downland Open Air Museum at Singleton. Here historic domestic and farm buildings peculiar to these uplands have been reconstructed. They include a wheelwright's shop, a granary store and a charcoal burner's camp. Like Pulborough's course, the museum nestles in among wooded slopes and a visit here is a superb complement to a day spent at what is undoubtedly the golfing jewel of the Downs.

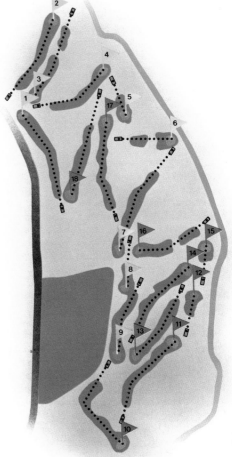

# Beauport Park and Rye

Beauport Park, St Leonards on
Sea, Hastings, East Sussex
*Tel: Hastings (0424) 52977*

Rye, Camber, Rye, Sussex
*Tel: Camber (079 75) 241*

Beauport Park
From Hastings drive 3 miles north on
the A2100

Beautiful tree-lined parkland course:
6235yds, SSS70

Visitors welcome
*Professional:* S R Bassil

Rye

On A259 1 mile east of Rye, turn on to
Camber/Lydd Airport road for 2 miles

Exposed links course: 6483yds, SSS72
*Course designer:* Harry Colt, later
reconstructed by Sir Guy Campbell

Visitors welcome only by introduction
and restricted Thursdays, weekends and
Bank Holidays
*Professional:* P Marsh

Hotels: Beauport Park★★★ Hastings
*Tel: Hastings (0424) 51222*
(20 rm)

George★★ Rye
*Tel: Rye (079 73) 2114*
(22 rm)

Hope Anchor★★ Rye
*Tel: Rye (079 73) 2216*
(14 rm)

Yelton★ Hastings
*Tel: Hastings (0424) 422240*
(40 rm)

As East Sussex tails into Kent, across Romney's gloomy marshes, the county's sentinel is Rye, a walled hill town two miles inland from the sea. Once it played a part in history as one of the ancient towns of the Cinque Ports. It is on this very land that has encroached into the sea, by the side of the River Rother's mouth, that a fabled links has been established. The Rye course, not the least renowned for its university ties and student high jinks (and an annual match by golfing journalists), is certainly a course to see and if possible to play over. For Rye is one of Britain's more exclusive golfing delights.

However, this corner of East Sussex holds a golf location which is in complete contrast to Rye. At nearby Hastings is one of the most modern courses in Britain. It is a slice of the municipal parkland of Beauport Park that has been converted and designed by Frank Penninck to a championship standard that will surely soon be recognised as an extremely worthy tournament venue.

The wooded undulations of the Hastings environs are nowhere so well appreciated as from the highest points of Beauport Park. Opened in July 1973, Penninck's design cut into 200 acres of woodland and fulfilled a long-felt need among the town's golfers as the Downs and St Leonards' clubs had been closed down in the Fifties after recurrent financial crises.

It is a course design which has occasioned some controversy, however, much of which comes from the elderly players who have to face some steep climbs.

The fact that the course was a natural watershed also caused problems, but some small modifications to the original concept and a little drainage attention has now overcome them. In fact modern groundsmanship has settled the course in remarkably quickly, enabling Penninck's challenging vision to be accomplished.

Measuring 6250 yards from the back tees and 6073 yards from the medal tees, Beauport's par scores are 71 and 70 respectively. Many of the course's hazards are entirely natural, there being a considerable premium on accuracy along its tree-lined fairways, with quite dense undergrowth roughs. The introductory holes give little hint of what lies ahead.

The start is a gentle par 4 on which a good drive and a six iron should find the green. Now the ground begins to rise gradually for the 493-yard 2nd to the heights from which it is possible to see through and over the trees to the patchwork quilt of Kent's rich pastures. A strong visual and playing feature of the 382-yard 3rd are two sturdy Wellingtonias standing as if on sentry duty by the green.

Beauport Park's best hole is without doubt the par 4 12th. From a slightly angled tee the

*Romney, Hythe and Dymchurch Railway*

drive must be finely controlled as a stream runs to the right of the lie ready to catch any suggestion of a pushed or sliced shot.

An aspect of this modern design is that both the legs of the course start at the clubhouse which also has a spacious practice ground. In coping with drainage problems the layout permitted the interchange of the 8th and 17th holes and this, Beauport's penultimate fairway, has benefitted by some levelling and the creation of a dogleg to the right. Over such a raised course so near to the sea it would be unusual if the wind did not come into play. In fact, Penninck has avoided this difficulty. The trees form a good windbreak and valleys and defiles protect the golfer from unkind gusts.

Quite the reverse is true at Rye which is exposed to the full force of the prevailing

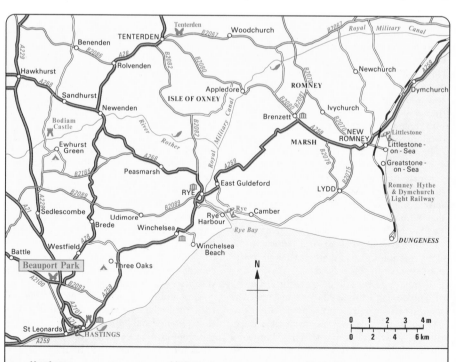

Hastings
*Tel: (0424) 52977*
Tree-lined seaside course, 18
holes, 6235yds, par 71, SSS70

Littlestone
*Tel: (067 93) 3355*
Flattish links course 1m SE of
New Romney, 18 holes,
6453yds, par 72, SSS71

Tenterden
*Tel: (058 06) 3987*
Pleasant parkland course, 9
holes, 5119yds, par 69, SSS65

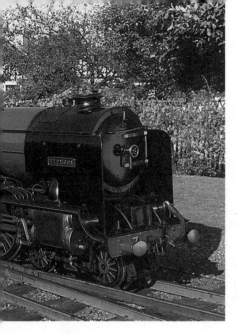

winds whipping across Rye Bay and devoid of protection from all other sides, too. It has played a part in many sterling battles since the course was first laid out in 1894 to a design by Harry Colt. He would fail to recognise it now, of course, since Sir Guy Campbell added nine new holes some years later and drew the course out along the estuary side of the Camber Road. A more modern modification was a completely new 10th. It is not just human designs that have changed Rye – near the end of the war, a doodlebug wiped out the old clubhouse.

Rye's lands drain fast and it is a popular winter club. Greens of fescue grass, well adapted to its salty diet, have a reputation for running very true and the fairway turf adds a distinct spring to your step. It is a tough turf and those used to more meadow-like fairways will find the going hard.

It is a course that has no par 5s and you will not gain much comfort from the five par 3s which are all of above-average length to make the second shot critical. It is the wind that makes all those par 4s the test they are. Highlights of Rye are the par 4 430-yard 4th with a fairway that perches like a narrow mountain road between dunes and a considerable drop; the sixth, a remeasured par 5, has a blind drive followed by a funnel through duneland. The blind Sea Hole (13th), brings the course almost fully into the wind. As a remote haven of the Oxford and Cambridge Golfing Society, Rye has a characterful tradition. Not the least is that the flatter part of the clubhouse roof is *not* out of bounds to those who hook their second shot on the 18th. It has never been lost to players that the 'quick' way from the 9th to the 10th tee is through the bar.

Hastings was not in fact the site of the 1066 battle – it was at Senlac (now renamed Battle, just up the road from Beauport Park) where William changed the course of British history. This popular resort town does have the stone from which it is said William ate his first meal on English soil and a 243-foot tapestry commemorating the 900th anniversary of

the event. A few small fishing boats are a reminder that this was one of the great Cinque Ports and the old town has net-drying sheds and a Fishermen's Museum. Hastings Country Park, to the east of the town, covers over 520 acres of clifftop walks, nature trails, picnic areas and the renowned beauty spot of Ecclesbourne Glen.

Hastings and its residential satellite, St Leonards, enjoy excellent sea fishing from shore marks such as Hooks Hard, the town pier and the harbour arm (from here to the East Groyne). Bass, cod, dab, mullet and whiting appear in catches. Camping is not so well catered for on this stretch of the coast, there being only two small sites, one of them almost next door to Beauport Park.

It is well worth a day trip from the area, through Rye to the wild tip of south west Kent at Dungeness. This is the terminal station of the Romney, Hythe and Dymchurch railway, a fourteen-mile trip pulled by scaled-down engines which are fully functional enough to have tugged an ack-ack battery up and down the line during the war. The railway is an ideal way to see the desolation of Romney Marshes.

It is a trip that could well give you the excuse to see the links of Rye, with its views across the Rother to Rye Harbour (a quaint mixture of ancient and modern port facilities), and the towers and castles on the skyline. These are a constant reminder that this coast was always considered to be Britain's Achilles heel as William once proved so well.

**BEAUPORT PARK GOLF COURSE**

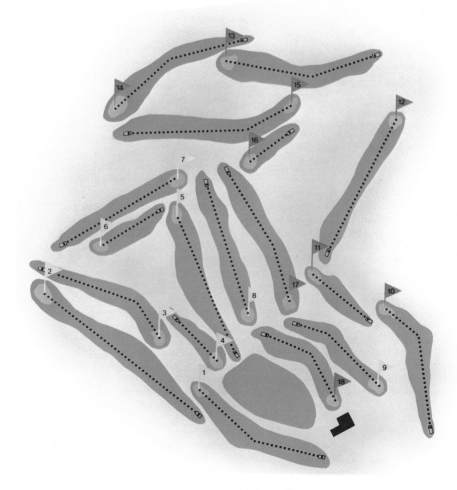

**Angling**
Hastings: shore fishing for bass, cod, mullet. Plus conger, pollack & tope by boat
River Rother (including Brede & Tillingham tributaries): coarse fishing plus occasional trout, with good access
Daily tickets:
C A Robins, 22 Landgate, Rye
*Tel: (079 73) 2150* or B Hart, Riverside Cottages, Newenden
Water Authority: SWA, Guildbourne House, Chatsworth Road, Worthing, Sussex
*Tel: (0903) 205252*
Royal Military Canal: fair coarse fishing, best in summer
Daily tickets: as River Rother
Water Authority: as River Rother

**Camping**
Ewhurst: Lordine Court Caravan Park ▶
*Tel: (058 083) 209*
Rural 120-pitch site (no caravans)
Open Easter–Oct, must book public holidays
Three Oaks: Old Coghurst Farm Caravan & Camping Park ▶▶▶
*Tel: (0424) 753622*
60-pitch woodland site 4m NE of Hastings
Open Mar–Oct, must

book Jul–Aug

**Walking Trails**
Ecclesbourne Glen: 1½m (2hr) signposted nature walk. Start from Barley Lane, Hastings

**General**
Brenzett: Brenzett Aeronautical Museum: many wartime planes including Spitfire, 8m NE of Rye
Open Easter–Oct Sun only, plus Tue, Wed & Thu afternoons Jul–Aug
*Tel: (058 06) 3197*
Dungeness: 'A' Nuclear Power Station
Open all year
*Tel: (0679) 20461*
Hastings: Hastings Castle: Norman fortress remains
Open Easter–Sep daily 10–5
St Clement's Caves: 4 acres of old smuggling caves
Open all year
*Tel: (0424) 422964*
Rye: Rye museum: 13th-century fortification housing Cinque Port, doll, shipbuilding & pottery items
Open Easter–mid-Oct daily
*Tel: (079 73) 3254*
Winchelsea: Winchelsea Museum: Cinque Port history plus maps & documents
Open May–Sep daily (ex Sun am)

# Royal Cinque Ports and Prince's

Royal Cinque Ports, Golf Road, Deal, Kent
*Tel: Deal (030 45) 4007*

Prince's, Prince's Drive, Sandwich Bay, Sandwich, Kent
*Tel: Sandwich (030 46) 2000*

---

Royal Cinque Ports

At north end of Deal's seafront off A258

Championship tees: 6645yds: Medal tees: 6384yds, SSS72

Visitors welcome with club introduction
*Professional:* I Morrison

Prince's

Off A256 (Upper Strand Street) 2 miles out of Sandwich

Blue Course: 6788yds, SSS72
9-hole: 3100yds, SSS35
*Course designers:* J S F Morrison and Sir Guy Campbell

Visitors welcome, reservation advisable
*Professional:* M Youngs

Hotels: Bell★★ Sandwich
*Tel: Sandwich (030 46) 2836*
(28 rm)

Court Stairs★★ Westcliff, Ramsgate
*Tel: Ramsgate (0843) 51850*
(17 rm)

San Clu★★ Ramsgate
*Tel: Ramsgate (0843) 52345*
(50 rm)

---

*Last shot of the day*

Kent offers the holiday or short-stay visitor an attraction shared by no other county in England or Scotland. It has three Open Championship courses – the Royal Cinque Ports, Deal, and Prince's and Royal St George's, Sandwich, nestling cheek by jowl on the county's eastern shore. This magnificent stretch of golfing country around the cross-channel hoverport of Pegwell Bay has been the setting of numerous triumphs and disasters dating as far back as J H Taylor's Open Championship victory at St George's in 1894. This was the first time the event had been played outside Scotland.

It was also at St George's in 1934 that Henry Cotton ended the Americans' post-war domination of the Open by winning the first of his three titles. Fifteen years later, that genial Irishman Harry Bradshaw was leading the field in the second round of the Open when he found his ball lodged in a broken bottle at the back of the fifth green. He elected to play it, smashed the bottle to get the ball out, but took a six for the hole. Bradshaw eventually tied with Bobby Locke and lost the play-off to the great South African. More recently an enormous audience on the grounds (and on television) watched Tony Jacklin hole-in-one on the 16th in the 1967 Dunlop Masters.

Royal St George's, to which the 1981 Open returns after a gap of thirty-two years, is unfortunately an all-male stronghold which offers few chances for visiting players. However, touring golfers of both sexes will find a warm welcome at Royal Cinque Ports (most people pronounce it 'sink'), Deal and the beautiful Prince's Course, both of which this report examines in more detail.

'Deal is a truly great course,' wrote the late Bernard Darwin, doyen of golf writers and a former captain of the club. 'This smiling corner of the earth's surface has for me something that no other spot, not even St Andrews, can quite equal'. Darwin went on to eulogise the testing nature of the course, the stunning view of the shining white cliffs rearing up beyond Pegwell Bay and the queue of ships visible from the clubhouse window.

The course was first played in 1892 along a north-south strip of foreshore which has a very downland character. A major feature of the course is a long rolling dune which humps up near the first green and is still making its presence felt on the long doglegs of the 10th and 11th holes. After a good drive up past the clubhouse at the 328-yard 1st, one has to negotiate a ditch which runs right across the fairway only a few yards short of the putting surface. It is a hole that sets the tone of the course. With a strong wind blowing it can take a couple of woods (or a wood and a long iron), calling for two perfectly struck shots.

At 199 yards, the par 3 14th, one of only three short holes at Deal, requires accurate club selection. Anything slightly left runs down into a grassy hollow, while if you miss the green on the right there are two big bunkers waiting to trap your tee shot. Misreading this green can easily cost three putts. Royal Cinque Ports, Deal, totals 6645 yards off the championship tees and 6384 yards off the medal tees, with a par of 70.

Prince's Sandwich has long catered for the holidaying and touring golfer and, indeed, players and non-golfers alike can book into the club's own 18-bedroom Dormy House for a package holiday. A new clubhouse is on the cards for this course, which was redesigned to its present layout in 1948 by a partnership between J S F Morrison and Sir Guy Cambell.

Situated literally on the beach, the Championship Blue Course measures 6800 yards but the holiday visitor may well prefer to play the nine-hole course of 3100 yards – it is demanding of skill but a more relaxing morning's round. This short course is the older part of Prince's grounds and still retains many pre-war features.

Of the many exacting facets of the Blue Course, memorable holes are the 5th and 17th. The 5th, at 433 yards is a dogleg to the left, with a long carry from the tee over a ridge into which is set a bunker, right in the middle of the fairway. Then a long iron second shot is required to reach a narrow green which falls away on both sides. The 411-yard 17th calls for a drive over the road and unless you hit a really good shot you will fail to reach the generous green. The putting surface is protected by a huge cross-bunker only ten yards short of the green perimeter. Even the best of golfers will be happy to come away from these two testing holes with par fours.

One delightful story of Prince's is that Wing Commander Laddie Lucas, a famous Battle of Britain fighter pilot, was actually born in the clubhouse. Some years later he found his local knowledge useful when, after a very hot dogfight over the Channel, he was able to land his damaged Spitfire at the far end of the course.

Both courses are close by the principal resort area of the Kent coast, a region known as Thanet. While Margate, Ramsgate and Broadstairs may draw much of Kent's tourist traffic, Deal itself and nearby Dover to the south have many attractions. At Deal there is a shelving beach of shingle and bathers are recommended to stay close to the shore on lifeguard-patrolled lengths of the shore. This is an ideal shore fishing location, however, and anglers also come to the area for the fishing from Deal's 1000-foot pier and charter boats operating from nearby Walmer to the wreck marks of the

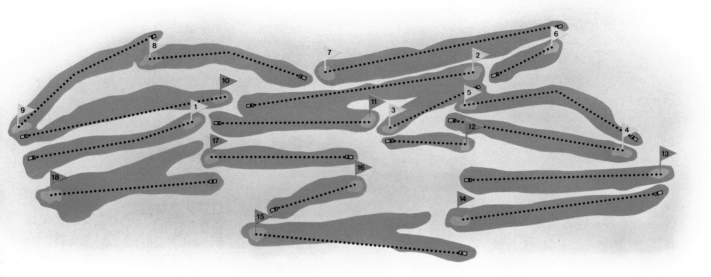

Goodwin sands. Deal has a maritime museum detailing the port's close associations with fishing and naval warfare, and Deal Castle, unusually built to the pattern of the Tudor rose, is open to the public. From Pegwell Bay's hoverport you can take cheap day trips to France without a passport.

The chalk cliffs of the area are the seaward face of the Kent downlands and these make ideal walking country. One arm of the waymarked North Downs Way explores the hinterland to the west of Deal and Dover. Sections of

the 141-mile path are accessible between Dover and Waldershare on the A256. This part of Kent is particularly badly off for nature trails but there are the West Woods Forest Walk near Elham and the trail on the Wye and Crundale Downs which is about two miles east of Wye on the A28.

Outdoor families will find that there are few campsites on the Sandwich-Deal stretch of the coast but several are centred on Dover itself and in the Isle of Thanet close to Ramsgate and Margate there are a number of sites.

Margate has all the attractions of a major family resort including the vast entertainments complex of Dreamland which has scenic rides, sideshows and a safari park. In contrast, Broadstairs and Ramsgate are more genteel havens. Broadstairs has strong Dickens connections, *the* Bleak House is on the town's north cliff and the author is celebrated in a small museum. Ramsgate, once the embarkation point for Wellington's troops (and more recently the recipient of returning Dunkirk heroes) is very much a sailing town with its excellent international marina and several competition events held by the Royal Temple Yacht Club.

Just a leisurely two-hour journey from London and a hop off the ferries from France, the golfing citadels of Kent make an ideal base for a few days of quiet relaxation for long-stay or continent-bound tourists alike.

**Canterbury:**
*Tel: (0227) 63586*
Rolling parkland course. 18 hole, 6222yds, par 70, SSS70
*Professional: T Bowden*

**Herne Bay:**
*Tel: (022 73) 3964*

5364yds, par 68, SSS66
*Professional: D I Brown*

**North Foreland (Broadstairs):**
*Tel: (0843) 62140*

Scenic seaside course. 18 hole, 6378yds, par 71, SSS70
*Professional: D Bonthron*

**Royal St George's (Sandwich):**
*Tel: (030 46) 3090*
(Men only) links course. 18 hole, 6539yds, par 70, SSS73
*Professional: C Whiting*

**St Augustine's (Ramsgate):**
*Tel: (0843) 821346*
Fairly flat seaside course. 18 hole, 5018yds, par 69, SSS65
*Professional: H Sherman*

**Walmer & Kingsdown (Deal):**
*Tel: (030 45) 3256*
Clifftop course with fine views. 18 hole, 6488yds, par 73, SSS71
*Professional: M Lee*

**Westgate & Birchington:**
*Tel: (0843) 31115*
Short links course. 18 hole, 4926yds, par 68, SSS65
*Professional: R Game*

**Angling**
Deal: shore & boat fishing for bass, cod, flounder, sole, whiting
Tackle shop: The Angler, 19 King Street
*Tel: (030 45) 4573*
Margate: excellent shore fishing for cod, dab, mullet, plaice, tope. By boat may add conger, bream, ray, turbot
Tackle shop: Geoff's Fishing Tackle, 36 Fort Hill
*Tel: (0843) 26386*
River Stour: coarse fish plus sea trout, but chances limited
Free fishing from Sandwich to estuary
Water Authority: SWA, Guildbourne House, Chatsworth Road, Worthing
*Tel: (0903) 205252*

**Camping**
Deal: Sutton Vale Caravan Park ▶▶▶
*Tel: (01 837) 1093*
*(Mon–Fri)*
Small 28-pitch site (no tents)

Open Apr–Sep, must book Jul–Aug
Minster: Wayside Caravan Park ▶▶
*Tel: (0843) 821272*
Compact 10-pitch site (no tents)
Open Mar–Oct, no bookings

**General**
Bekesbourne: Howletts Zoo Park: large collection of wild animals 4m SE of Canterbury
Open all year daily 10–6
Canterbury: Roman Pavement: section of Roman house plus local exhibits
Open Apr–Sep Mon–Fri (plus Oct–Mar afternoons only)
*Tel: (0227) 52747*
Deal: Deal Castle: 16th-century stronghold with pottery & Iron Age weapon exhibits
Open all year
Reculver: Roman Fort: remains of 3rd-century fort.
Accessible all year

# Aldeburgh

Aldeburgh, Suffolk
*Tel: Aldeburgh (072 885) 2890*

---

7 miles east of Aldeburgh off A12 via Farnham

Two links courses: Championship course: 6344yds, SSS70; River Course: 2114yds, SSS32

Visitors welcome with club introduction
*Professional:* R Knight

Hotels: Brudenell★★★ Aldeburgh
*Tel: Aldeburgh (072 885) 2071*
(47 rm)

Wentworth★★★ Aldeburgh
*Tel: Aldeburgh (072 885) 2312*
(33 rm)

White Lion★★★ Aldeburgh
*Tel: Aldeburgh (072 885) 2720*
(32 rm)

---

Suffolk's coast has been perpetually under attack. It is a land of dunes, enormously pebbly beaches, wooded foreshores and marshy hinterlands which has been fought over by many of Britain's invaders. It is also a shore that has constantly changed its shape in retreat from the advancing sea. Aldeburgh grew to something like its present size when the shipyards of Slaughdon and the entire village were engulfed by the sea. It was at Slaughdon that the Reverend George Crabbe wrote *The Borough*, a collection of stories which inspired Benjamin Britten to write *Peter Grimes*. For Aldeburgh was this great composer's home town and it is his dedication which gave the area the important cultural event of the Aldeburgh Festival held in the Maltings at nearby Snape.

For nearly a hundred years, Aldeburgh has meant golf on a course that, although now one

and a half miles inland, was undoubtedly once a part of the shore. Here are all the features of a classic sandy links, with sea turf overlaid by the first markers of heathland, the bright gorse, and clumps of trees. Laid out by persons unknown, today's course has been little changed over the years and the fact that it withstands the wear and tear of today's playing techniques and the club's popularity bear testimony to the skill with which its grounds have been superintended over the years. Indeed, Aldeburgh is renowned for the condition of its turf on both greens and fairways. It is a short course for a championship venue, but none the less demanding in skill and, of course, its 6366 yards from the back tees make an extremely satisfying holiday round.

Played in a triangle of ground between the main A1094 Saxmundham road and the B1122, Aldeburgh's course begins, centres and ends around the clubhouse, which has views of the 2nd, 9th and 18th greens as well as the 1st and 10th tees. Aldeburgh tees off for a stiff par 4 of 407 yards played from an elevated tee to a green that is modestly banked. You can relax a little more on the second as it should be possible to carry its 367 yards in two round the slight left-hand dogleg and down a slope to a large green. The course starts uphill again for the 3rd, justifying its par 4 with not inconsiderable gorse roughs and a green that is beset by bewildering bunkers.

A kidney green is a feature of the first of Aldeburgh's short holes, sited behind a great sleepered bunker which extends round to the right. The flag can be at the back of the green near to further bunkers and while the 4th's 140-yard length will not intimidate, finding the green in one will.

With the next three holes you will really begin to earn your score. At par 4 apiece, they are all over 400 yards, the 5th in particular being a great driver's hole at 440 yards. Shave as close to the left as you can to get a clear entry to the green. The 6th is only mildly less severe – a dogleg of over 430 yards – while the 7th has

a cross-bunker judged just right for the indeterminate drive at about 180 yards along the fairway. Do not expect any quarter from the short 8th, as the green is elusive over a 165-yard shot and there is a road hazard. As often as not, an easterly wind makes the choice of club perilous. If you do not get the wind on the 8th it comes into play on the 9th back to the clubhouse – a modest 383-yard par 4 from an elevated tee over considerable gorse.

There is a temptation here to revive flagging fortunes and well-being with an interlude in the bar before embarking on Aldeburgh's superb second leg. The 10th is a good pace-setter at 421 yards for the par 4 which features some heavy cross-bunkering of the fairway and a green set in a hollow ringed by dunes and bunkers. Open your shoulders a bit for the long carry required on the drive of the 11th, a more severe par 4 of 469 yards. A good drive and a short iron may suffice on the 324 yards of the 12th but that is only if you clear the cavernous cross-bunker and find the tricky green. The Leiston Road boundary threatens on the dogleg of the 13th before you come to grips with the splendid quality of the 14th, a 361-yard par 4 doglegging between a pair of guardian trees. About 200 yards out, at just that distance which requires some careful thought, is a ridge of sand crossing the fairway. The green is

**CHAMPIONSHIP COURSE**

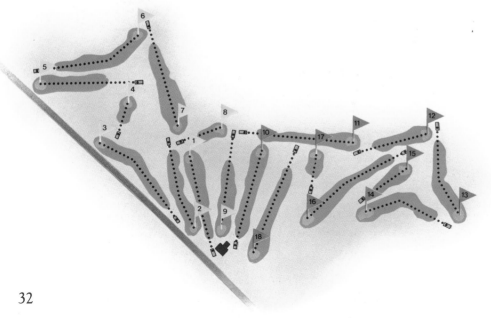

**Angling**
Aldeburgh: shore fishing for cod, dab, plaice, sole & whiting. Boat fishing very limited
River Deben: fair for perch & roach
Daily tickets: The Rod & Gunshop, 62 Thoroughfare, Woodbridge
*Tel: (039 43) 2377*
Water Authority: AWA, Diploma House, Grammar School Walk, Huntingdon
*Tel: (0480) 56181*

**Camping**
Leiston: King George's Caravan Park ▶▶
*Tel: (0728) 830129*
Level 18-pitch site (no tents) 5m N of Aldeburgh
Open Apr–Oct, must book Bank Holidays
Shottisham: St Margaret's Guest House ▶
*Tel: (039 441) 247*
Grassy 25-pitch site near estuary
Open Apr–Oct, must book Jul–Aug

**Walking Trails**
Easton Farm Park Nature Trail: ¾m (⅔hr) signposted walk through riverside woodland. Start 1½m NW of Wickham

Market, Woodbridge

**General**
Aldeburgh: Moot Hall: restored 16th-century timbered building
Open Easter–Oct times vary
*Tel: (072 885) 2158*
Dunwich: Dunwich Museum: interesting relics of local history
Open all year Sat & Sun only (plus Tue & Thu during summer)
*Tel: (072 873) 218/276*
Leiston: Leiston Abbey: extensive remains of 14th-century abbey
Accessible all year
Letheringham: Watermill & Gardens: 250-year-old mill in 4-acre gardens & park, 2m NW of Wickham Market
Open Easter–Sep times vary
*Tel: (0728) 746349*
Orford: Orford Castle: unusual triple-towered 12th-century fortress
Open all year
Saxmundham: Glemham Hall: 17th-century house in 350-acre grounds, 3m W of Saxmundham
Open mid-Apr–Sep Wed & Sun pm
*Tel: (0728) 746219*

elevated and attaining it will need very careful club selection.

A fearsome par 3 follows. The confident who will hope to make it a one-shotter for its 201 yards again fall in that middle ground that sorts the men from the boys. For some, Aldeburgh's 16th will be among the great driving holes for its 457-yard length demands two formidable shots. The first must carry the slight left-hand dogleg, while the second must overstep or dodge a wicked cross-bunker short of the green.

Aldeburgh ends with a bang rather than a whimper on a 142-yard par 3, demanding immaculate marksmanship both to find the green and avoid the belligerent bunker, of full Aldeburgh size, sitting open-jawed before the green. The final hole is a worthy championship finisher of 424 yards, par 4 with a tightening approach to the green from a far from expansive fairway.

Gentler souls, or holiday-makers seeking a little less stimulus from their play will also welcome Aldeburgh's 9-hole River Course played down to the River Alde on the opposite side of the Saxmundham road.

There is more idle sport to be had along the coastline where the beaches continually change and beachcombing can be a fascinating diversion – finds of cornelian and amber are not uncommon. While offshore, a lively sea attracts yachtsmen, smaller sail boats tend to stick to the gentler waters of the mere at Woodbridge (where boats may also be hired). A mile away at Sutton Hoo Ship Burial, are the remains of a Saxon ship which was discovered, with a hold full of treasure, in 1939.

This area has its fair share of Royal connections. Mary Tudor lived at Framlingham Castle for a time and at Orford Henry II built the eighteen-sided castle which looks out to the Ness and lighthouse.

It is impossible to say when the first mill was built at Letheringham, but one is mentioned in the Doomsday Book and the watermill there today is 250 years old. It is surrounded by acres of woodland and gardens with riverside picnic spots.

Anglers have the choice of coarse fish in the Deben or the shore marks along the Aldeburgh coast. Perhaps best of all is Dirty Wall, for bass, mullet, sole and whiting. Since this coastline is officially an area of Outstanding Natural Beauty, and the countryside is generally flat, it is ideal for lazy walks. A most rewarding place for bird-watching is Minsmere Nature Reserve near Dunwich. On the beaches backed by low cliffs and heathland are many rare species – an invigorating five and a half-mile walk encompasses the reserve.

Campers and caravanners have little choice in sites; the largest, with twenty-eight pitches, is at Waldringfield.

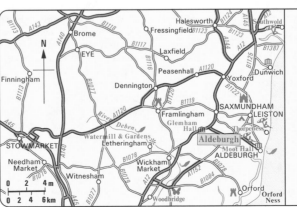

**Southwold**
*Tel: (050 272) 3234*
Commonland course with sea views, 9 holes, 6023yds, par 70, SSS68
*Professional: B. Allen*

**Thorpeness (Aldeburgh)**
*Tel: (072 885) 2176*
Moorland course with natural hazards, 18 holes, 6208yds, par 69, SSS70
*Professional: W Cattell*

**Woodbridge**
*Tel: (039 43) 2038*
Very fine upland course, 18 holes, 6297yds, par 70, SSS70
*Professional: L Jones*

# Hunstanton

Hunstanton, Norfolk
*Tel: Hunstanton (048 53) 2811*

From Hunstanton drive ½ mile on A149

Seaside links course: 6670yds, SSS72
*Course designer:* James Braid

Visitors welcome but restricted at
weekends and Bank Holidays
*Professional:* J Carter

Hotels: Le Strange Arms★★ Old
Hunstanton
*Tel: Hunstanton (048 53) 2810*
(28 rm)

Lodge★ Hunstanton
*Tel: Hunstanton (048 53) 2896*

Manor★★ Titchwell
*Tel: Brancaster (048 521) 221*
(6 rm)

It would be surprising if such a long coast of
natural dunelands as that of Norfolk and East
Anglia did not have its string of links of sterling quality. Indeed, there is scattering of clubs
on this coast – but not so many of them. The
reason is undoubtedly that the flat agricultural
hinterland was never very crowded and is becoming increasingly depopulated. What demand there is for good golf arises close to the
major population centres such as King's Lynn
and Norwich. That is how the links courses are

**Angling**
Hunstanton: shore
fishing for bass, dab,
mackerel & ray. Plus
cod & dogfish from
boats

**Camping**
Fakenham:
Crossways Caravan
Park ▶▶▶
*Tel: (032877) 335*
Flat 25-pitch site (no
tents) 3m E of
Fakenham
Open Apr–Sep, must
book Jul–Aug
Hunstanton: Searles
Camping Ground ▶
*Tel: (048 53) 2342*
Grassy 135-pitch site
(75 tents)
Open Apr–Sep, must
book Jul–Aug

**Riding**
Beeston: Street
Farm Stables (Ms E
Coulson), Beeston,
Litcham
*Tel: (032876) 286*
Hunstanton: The
Children's Christian
Riding Centre (Rev L
Park), 'Flaxley',
Holme, Hunstanton
*Tel: (048525) 216*

**Walking Trails**
Jocelyn's Wood: ¾m
(½ hr) woodland walk.
Start from car park at
Sandringham Park,
8m N of King's Lynn
Scolt Head Island:

¼m (¾hr) signposted
walk through sea-bird
reserve. Start from
Brancaster Staithe
Harbour (1½m ferry
trip) off A149

**General**
Burnham Market:
Carmelite Friary:
ruins of 13th-century
abbey. Accessible all
year
*Tel: (0603) 611122
ext 5224*
Holkham: Holkham
Hall: fine 18th-
century Palladian
mansion in large
grounds 2m W of
Wells-next-the-Sea
Open Jun–Sep Thu
(plus Mon Jul–Aug)
Hunstanton: Norfolk
Lavender: largest
lavender-growing
centre in Britain, 3m
S of Hunstanton at
Heacham
*Tel: (0485) 70384*
King's Lynn: Castle
Rising: fine Norman
keep & earthwork 5m
N of King's Lynn
Open all year
Sandringham:
Sandringham House
& Grounds: 19th-
century royal
residence with small
museum
Open Apr–Sep (ex Fri
& Sat – & Jul 21–Aug
9)
*Tel: (0553) 2675*

34

## Map

```
0  1  2  3  4 m
0  2  4  6 km
```

**Fakenham**
*Tel: (0328) 2867*
Parkland course with many water
hazards, 9 holes, 5636yds, par 70,
SSS67
*Professional:* R Parry

**King's Lynn**
*Tel: (055 387) 654*
Modern (opened 1975) woodland
course 4m NE of King's Lynn, 18
holes, 6529yds, par 72, SSS71
*Professional:* C Hanlon

**Royal West Norfolk**
*Tel: (048521) 223*
Traditional seaside course 7m E
of Hunstanton off A149, 18 holes,
6222yds, par 70, SSS70
*Professional:* R A Kimber

distributed. There are the wonderful pair at
Hunstanton and Brancaster (the Royal West
Norfolk) close to King's Lynn and nothing
much more until Cromer, close to Norwich.

Hunstanton, the only east coast resort
which faces west because it is sited on the cusp
of Norfolk as it dips into the Wash, has a
course laid out along the foreshore, north of
the town that was established in 1891. The
club's records show the original 9-holes, now
almost completely indiscernible, cost just £150
and the extension to 18 holes in 1895 was an
even better bargain at £25. Much of today's
course owes its shape to James Braid, who
burrowed around in the sand to produce a set of
bunkers that are the course's most formidable
hazard. Of Braid's excavations, Bernard Darwin wrote: 'He left a most destructive trail of
bunkers behind him; wonderfully cunningly
devised they are so that if we narrowly avoid
one we are very likely to be caught in another
. . . just as we were rejoicing at our unmerited
escape'. In fact, Braid allowed for twenty more
bunkers but the committee had an eye to their
own handicaps and politely declined.

Hunstanton is the scene of R J Taylor's golfing miracle of 1974, when he holed in one at
the 188-yard, par 3, 16th on *three* days in
succession. He could not have experienced
very much wind which, at Hunstanton makes
all the difference between a game with room to
move and a nail-biting effort to stay on the
card at all.

Right from the 1st, Braid's work intrudes in
the shape of massive cross-bunker, set in a
sandy ridge about 150 yards from the tee on this
343-yard par 4 – it should be carried in one.

Broken in, by now you may be prepared to face
the course's longest hole, the 2nd of over 530
yards round a left hand dogleg that demands a
line to the right for an opening on the second
leg. The 3rd takes you in the opposite swing, a
dogleg of about 440 yards, considered to be one
of Hunstanton's great holes. The temptation is
to take the left course, but this will require a
very long second to stay up on the card –
shaving into the right, a thick rough, is a
potentially greater risk. This is after all a par 4.

A bit more loft than you would imagine
could carry over the bunkers guarding the 4th
but it is Hunstanton's old sea defences that
create the fun on the 5th. The green actually
lies beyond a gap cut in an old sea wall, so the
second shot has to be spot-on.

Final hole of the first leg is the demanding
500 yards-plus of the par 5 9th, which doglegs
back towards the clubhouse as the ground becomes noticeably more broken towards the sea.
It is nowhere near as searching as the 11th,
which is another blockbuster of nearly a quarter of a mile for a par 4. Never mind the view
over the beach from the high tee – you must
drive down a narrowing defile to an elevated
green. The 12th is something of a relief, head-
ing inland over a hummock in the fairway.
There is also a blind crest to the 13th and
many's the visitor who must have gasped after
passing the guide post to see the set of hills and
hollows that must be cleared with the second.
You may also feel it is splitting hairs to have a
par 5 15th of 476 yards, albeit a dogleg around a
cavernous bunker, and grant a mere 446 yards
par 4 on the 17th when there is another bunker
at the turn here. Hunstanton's 18th keeps up

tension to the last, with a drive along a shallow valley that must be carried on to the green with the second if there is to be a chance of making par 4 on the final putts.

If you are a water-sports enthusiast, Hunstanton will hold even more appeal. It is a centre for water-ski-ing and sailing and many holidaymakers to the area tow their own boats to the slip-way – a day ticket is obtainable from the local Power Boat Club. The less intrepid can sunbathe on miles of sandy beach under curiously striped cliffs, take a donkey ride, or an organised boat trip from the harbour – notably a two-hour visit to Seal Island.

Play the course at Hunstanton in August and

the non-golfing members of the family have a treat in store at Caley Mill, Heacham. It is a converted grain mill that is surrounded by a sea of lavender, where visitors can walk among acres of the mauve, pungent harvest and watch the process which converts the flowers to perfumes and soaps.

Walkers are on the doorstep of the ancient Peddar's Way which runs south from Ringstead near Holme-next-the-Sea. The shores of the Wash are a spotting-ground for species of sea-birds and wildfowl, while sea-anglers can take a boat out of King's Lynn for catches of cod, conger and ray.

King's Lynn is at its liveliest on Tuesdays –

market day – and during its annual Festival of Music and Arts in July. Wedgwood glass is made on the Hardwicke estate and visitors can watch the craftsmen at work and buy a decanter afterwards. But perhaps the only 'must' is a visit to the Queen's country retreat at Sandringham.

The elegant house, bought by Queen Victoria for the Prince of Wales, is open to the public throughout the year except when the royal family take *their* summer break. If there were, today, a golfing monarch, the family would be hard put to choose between Brancaster and Hunstanton, but the latter would probably have it by a short head.

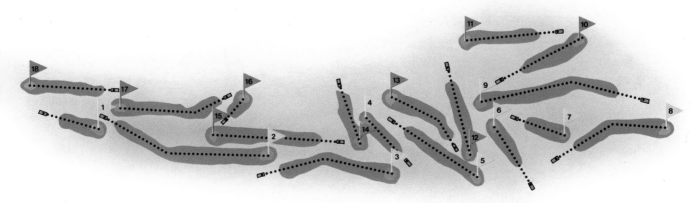

# Woodhall Spa

## Woodhall Spa, Lincolnshire
*Tel: Woodhall Spa (0526) 52511*

10 miles south west of Horncastle on B1191

Flat heathland course: 6831yds, SSS73
*Course designer:* H S Colt, later reconstructed by Colonel S V Hotchkin

Visitors welcome by prior telephone appointment
*Professional:* A Fixter

Hotels: Golf★★ Woodhall Spa
*Tel: Woodhall Spa (0526) 52434*
(57 rm)

Ladbroke Mercury Motor Inn★★★
Hornchurch
*Tel: Ingrebourne (040 23) 46789*
(145 rm)

Moor Lodge★★ Branston
*Tel: Lincoln (0522) 791366*
(31 rm)

Poised between the cathedral town of Lincoln and the brash resorts of the east coast is an oasis of golf in an almost flat and featureless plain of dyke-drained agricultural land. Among most golf writers' top six inland courses is Woodhall Spa, long ago the fount of health-giving waters and now the home of stimulating golf to a large and thriving club.

There have been two previous courses in the tree-veiled heathland of Woodhall Spa, the first dating back to 1894. On the present site a course designed by the famous rival champions Harry Vardon and James Braid was used from 1905. Virtually all eighteen holes were reconstructed only six years later by H S Colt but the course did not take its present form until shortly after the Great War. It was then that the owner of the club, Colonel S V Hotchkin, turned the land into one of the stiffest tests of golfing skill ever devised. So perfect was his design, that his son Neil Hotchkin, the present owner and President, has made very few minor alterations in the succeeding years. Colonel Hotchkin went on to assist in the design of both Ashridge and the West Sussex (see pages 26 and 27) and was involved in laying out several top-class South African courses.

Few who come from the South and drive through the Lincolnshire fens believe that they will find a village and such a course set in the midst of pine and birch woods. The land is comparatively flat, the turf springy and the soil is the result of glacial action – sand and gravel overlies Kimmeridge clay. The course drains very quickly and is generally in play for the whole year, there being important open competitions at Christmas and several other of the Bank Holidays.

The club has an extensive practice ground and in the summer months play is possible on a 9-hole pitch and putt course laid out on the other side of the old railway line behind the old-fashioned little clubhouse. In spring, gorse and broom bushes colour the course and later in the year the eye is drawn to banks of rhododendrons. Autumn brings out the heather and ling in subtle contrast to the changing hues of the trees and bracken.

Woodhall Spa is no course for the beginner, only those players of considerable experience can meet its challenge. The first hole looks deceptively easy, however, its 358 yards not a long carry from the tee and it has a moderately wide fairway. The second does demand more attention, for while there is little to deter the player in the vista from the tee, there is a line of bunkers to catch the slice matched by a huge trap waiting for the hook. The entry to the green is formidably narrow. At the third, Woodhall really begins to show its teeth, the player having little chance of getting away with a topped drive. There are trees to the right and an enticing rough of heather to the left. From this hole onwards the fairway must be found with every shot; taking the ball straight up the middle is the only way to keep the card on an even keel.

Woodhall greens are all fairly expansive but each has a very narrow approach and seventeen of them are set about with bunkers. Accuracy is essential – the wild hitter will never find himself on the fairway. In fact the course has nearly ninety bunkers, the extent of very few being immediately visible.

The short holes 5, 8 and 12 (155 yards, 198 yards and 151 yards respectively) differ greatly from one another but all are testing, being particularly well-bunkered. Drives at the 414-yard dogleg 7th and at the 447-yard 11th need particular care. The latter marks the turn back to the clubhouse and is particularly prone to cross-winds hurtling the ball into a road out of bounds, or even over Sandy Lane. The 12th doubles back again to a high green.

The round is completed by a wicked set of three par 4s and a par 5. The 15th is quite delightful, with some hazards on the fairway taking you to a green set in a basin surrounded by bunkers. An area of undulating ground guards the green of the 16th, sending balls all over the place, a difficulty repeated on the 17th. At 327 yards this might not appear to be a great par 4 but most players do consider it the

most testing of Woodhall's many distractions. The green is slightly elevated, with undulations very close to the hole itself. The 18th, at 493 yards, with the Colonel's oak tree standing guard and the mid-way cross bunkers barring access to a green that falls away from the

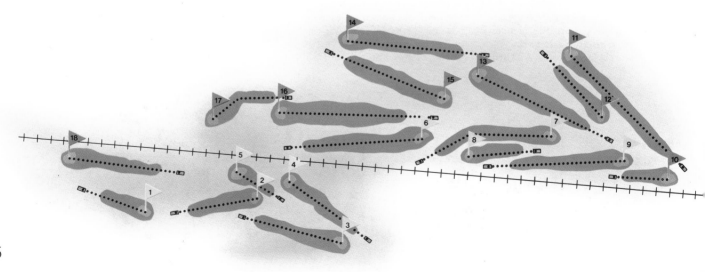

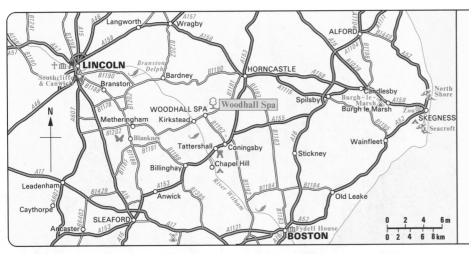

**Blankney**
Tel: (0526) 20263
Quiet parkland course 10m SE of
Lincoln off B1188, 18 holes, 6302yds, par 70,
SSS70

**North Shore (Skegness)**
Tel: (0754) 3298
Easily walked parkland course, 18 holes, 6010yds,
par 71, SSS69
*Professional: R Squires*

**Seacroft (Skegness)**
Tel: (0754) 3020
Flattish links course, 18 holes, 6478yds, par 71,
SSS71
*Professional: J cornelius*

**Southcliffe & Canwick
(Lincoln)**
Tel: (0522) 22166
Good parkland course, 18 holes, 5523yds, par 68,
SSS67

front apron, makes a fine end to this course.

Woodhall's membership is fairly low at about 450. Many of the players are drawn from all over Lincolnshire and parts of the North where play is not possible over the winter months. The club has hosted many of the major amateur events of the last decade, including the English Amateur, the Brabazon, the Ladies' Home Internationals and the British Youths' Championship. More recently it was the venue for the 1980 British Ladies' Amateur Open and the 1981 Men's Home International.

It is worth recording the history of Woodhall Spa itself. This popular watering place boasts a pump-room and baths for those who believe the therapeutic claims for the mineral water arising here. It is thought that the prominent 60-foot Tower-on-the-Moor may have been erected by the builders of nearby Tattershall Castle in the 15th century. It is matched by a tall column surmounted by the bust of Wellington set alongside the Horncastle road in 1844. The column overlooks Waterloo Wood, which results from the commemorative planting of acorns after the battle of 1815.

Woodhall Spa has a small caravan-only site but the nearest tenting site is at Chapel Hill on the River Witham, eight miles away.

Much of the tourist traffic in this area heads for Skegness, twenty-four miles from Woodhall. It is a predominantly modern resort, although its history stretches back to the Danish invasions. The town, much loved by Alfred Lord Tennyson, derives its name from that of the chief of the invaders – 'Skeggi'. Sea angling is particularly good from Gibraltar Point to the Seacroft beach and off the sea defences at Ingoldmells. You can take boats from Skegness and Boston to the south for fishing in deep water which yields cod, dogfish, mackerel, ray, tope and whiting. Bait can be dug on local beaches.

Gibraltar Point is a nature reserve with several trails to fascinate the nature-loving walker. A large bird population lives on a natural habitat of saltmarsh sand dunes and sand cliffs. Only ten miles north of Skegness and five miles inland is the contrasting habitat of Well Vale near Alford. This 18th-century house has a fascinating nature trail of two miles over mature woodlands and

plantations set out attractively around a lake.

Between Skegness and Woodhall stretch the fenlands of Lincolnshire, which owe much to the Dutch for drainage systems and an undeniable cultural influence. It is all the more surprising then to come across Woodhall Spa in your drive inland. In an area vastly under-rated for its scenic beauty, this superb course breaks the countryside between the wolds in the north and the great plain of the south, giving you all the more reason to go out of your way for a round of golf, at its best in such tranquillity.

**Angling**
Branston Delph: short land drain offering good coarse fishing
Daily tickets: Witham & District Joint Anglers' Federation (R Hobley), 30 Gunby Avenue, Lincoln
Tel: (0522) 683688
River Witham (lower): good bream with fair access
Daily tickets (for Tattershall area): on bank
Water Authority: AWA (Lincs Rivers Division), Diploma House, Grammar School Walk, Huntingdon
Tel: (0480) 56181

**Camping**
Chapel Hill: Orchards Caravans ►►►
Tel: (0526) 42414
Grassy 33-pitch site 3m S of Coningsby
Open Jun–Oct, must book Jul–Aug
Skegness: Richmond Drive Carapark ►►►
Tel: (0754) 2097
Level 100-pitch site (no tents)
Open Apr–mid-Sep, must book Jul–Aug

**Walking Trails**
Gibraltar Point Nature Reserve: 2m (1½hr) circular wildlife walk. Start from Skegness car park (south) on A52. Well Vale Nature Trail: 2m (1½hr) signposted woodland walk. Start from crossroads 1½m

SW of Alford on A1104.

**General**
Boston: Fydell House: 18th-century Georgian house
Open Mon–Fri 10–6 during term time
Tel: (0205) 63116
Guildhall: 16th-century building housing museum & art gallery
Open all year (ex Sun)
Tel: (0205) 64601
Lincoln: Lincoln Castle: Norman motte & bailey stronghold
Open all year (ex Sun pm)
Tel: (0522) 25951
Usher Gallery: collection of water-colours, miniatures & ceramics
Open all year (ex Sun pm)
Tel: (0522) 27980
Skegness: Burgh-le-Marsh Windmill: 19th-century 5-sailed tower windmill in working order, 5m W of Skegness off A158
Tel: (0754) 810281
Skegness Natureland Marine Zoo: modern marine zoo & sanctuary
Open all year daily 10–7.30 (10–4 in winter)
Tel: (0754) 4345
Tattershall: Tattershall Castle: well-restored keep of 15th-century fortified house
Open all year daily 11–6.30 (Sun 1–6.30)

# Berkshire, Sunningdale and Wentworth

Berkshire, Swinley Road, Ascot, Berkshire
*Tel: Ascot (0990) 21495/6*

Sunningdale, Ridgmount Road, Sunningdale, Berkshire
*Tel: Ascot (0990) 21681*

Wentworth, Virginia Water, Surrey
*Tel: Wentworth (099 04) 2201*

Berkshire

Between Ascot and Bagshot on A332

Two heathland courses: Red Course: 6356yds, SSS70; Blue Course: 6258yds, SSS70

Visitors welcome, reservation advisable
*Professional:* K A MacDonald

Sunningdale

To east of A30 near Sunningdale level crossing

Two wooded heath courses: Old Course: 6336yds, SSS70 (*Designer:* Willie Park); New Course: 6601yds, SSS70 (*Designer:* H Colt)

Visitors welcome on weekdays with reservation
*Professional:* C Clark

Wentworth

To east of A30 at Virginia Water

Two wooded heath and park courses
West course: 6969yds, SSS73
East course: 6184yds, SSS69

Visitors welcome on weekdays with reservation
*Professional:* B Gallacher

Hotels: Berystede★★★ Sunninghill
*Tel: Ascot (0990) 23311*
(96 rm)

Royal Foresters★★ Ascot
*Tel: (034 47) 4747*

Few newcomers to London and the south-western fringes of the city will realise that there is a broad belt of inhospitable country stretching from the northern part of Surrey almost continuously around a quarter of the capital to the Thames. Composed of heathland, with heather, gorse and the occasional rocky promontary, it is not surprising that the area has concealed in it some very fine golf courses. Some twenty-five miles from London, deep in the stockbroker belt, are three of the best inland courses in Britain. Little more than a drive and a pitch apart are the two that will need no introduction to golf fans – Sunningdale and Wentworth. The third is a close neighbour, the Berkshire.

Of the three, Berkshire is the youngest, being founded in 1928. Herbert Fowler laid out both of the courses here, the Red and the Blue. The Berkshire escapes international attention because it is a stated policy of the club to eschew professional events – but two major competitions in the amateur calendar held here are the Berkshire Trophy and the Avia Women's International Foursomes. Both courses top 6250 yards (Red, 6356 yards: Blue 6258 yards) and the club's grounds extend over 370 acres of heathland off the A332 between Ascot and Bagshot. Unusually, the Red and the Blue are considered to be of equal character and difficulty – where they differ is that the Red is on slightly higher ground.

Notable holes on the Red, amongst its odd mix of six par 3s and six par 5s, are the 10th, 16th and 17th. The 10th is a short dogleg across an avenue with a length of 187 yards and a considerable drop away to the right. A tree-lined fairway leads up to the 16th, demanding pinpoint accuracy to avoid the many bunkers and a good deal of loft to get over the slope to the green. You hardly have time to take breath before the 529-yard assault course of the 17th, which will take two really strong swings through trees to get a crack at the double decker green.

Drama comes early on the Blue Course. The first hole tees off under the gaze of members in the clubhouse waiting for over-ambitious newcomers to strike out for the green which looks invitingly near. In fact it is over 200 yards away and the intervening ground falls away to a clump of trees with some good patches of heather to cost a shot or two. There are more of these sort of temptations on every hole until you reach the renowned 16th.

Dizzily long for a par 4, at 452 yards, the fairway is beset by one seemingly enormous left hand bunker to foil a short drive and a rise to compete with on your second shot. Throughout both courses, the plentiful tree cover and exhilarating terrain places the utmost demand on accuracy.

Sunningdale needs very little introduction to professionals and armchair golfers alike. Of the two courses, the Old and the New, the Old Course is the one that regularly flashes across the television screen as the venue for the European LPGA championship. Both are carved from heavily tree-covered ground, the Old at 6336 yards being designed by Willie Park and the New, slightly longer at 6601 yards, was commissioned in 1922 from the famed Harry Colt.

Playing the Old Course is the major Sunningdale experience. Long carries over heather, strategically placed bunkers, a picturesque pond at the 5th that seems to attract your second shot like a magnet and the ever-present threat of the trees are the main features. That is ignoring the superb greens with burrows that defy reading.

If you have managed to keep your card in shape, it is the last four holes that will really

*The Berkshire*

make or break it and determine your fortune.

The 15th, a beguiling par 3 and a length of 226 yards is a wolf in sheep's clothing – when you do reach the green you find it is uncommonly large, but it is a devil to find among its cohort of bunkers. The 16th (423 yards par 4) has a bunch of hidden bunkers strung down the right hand side to catch the drive and a further row across the fairway at about 140 yards to catch your second shot.

More accuracy is called for at the 17th, a 421-yard right hand dogleg with a hard-earned par 4. Push your drive and you will find bunkers to the right – head off left and the way is blocked by trees. The second shot is longer than it may at first appear and you have to go in to the left to take full advantage of the green's considerable slope.

One of the most famous finishing holes in golf, the 18th is only slightly shorter than the previous pair with its green backed by an imposing oak tree and the clubhouse in the middle distance. This is a long uphill hole, formidable for its great bar of bunkers just short of the hole and even more traps around the green itself.

Among every professional's selection of the best eighteen holes of competitive golf must be Bobby Jones' 66 put up on this course during the climax to the 1927 Open Championship qualifying round.

More akin in character to Sunningdale than the Berkshire, Wentworth is again sculpted in great avenues between thick woods. That is where the similarity ends. Whereas Sunningdale makes every attempt to lure players into a

false sense of security, there is no doubt about the challenge of every single one of Wentworth's West Course holes, particularly those which form stepping stones in the famous hairpin avenue of Burma Road.

Wentworth is to all addicts the home of the World Matchplay Championship. So august is its history, that these fade into oblivion by the side of all the other Wentworth firsts. This is the seat of the Ryder Cup, a series dreamed up after tryouts at Gleneagles and Wentworth in the early Twenties. The East Course saw the first battles of the Curtis Cup in 1932 and it has been a noted location for Canada/World Cup skirmishes.

The West Course was designed by Harry Colt with his partners John Morrison and Charles Alison, while it was Colt alone who takes the credit for the lesser-known East Course. The East Course should not be lightly dismissed as the resort of amateurs wishing to claim a Wentworth card. It has a fine complement of five short holes to match any on the West Course and a tough three finishing holes.

Anyone with a bit of attack will want to play the Burma Road, however – the challenge of 6969 yards of golf at its finest just has to be experienced to be believed. Marvel at the event which made the 155-yard par 3 second hole the most famous place in the golfing world – here Isao Aoki won a £40 000 house by holing in one in 1979. That is ignoring the fact that you have to make par 4 over the 471 yards of the first fairway.

As at Sunningdale, Wentworth also has a healthy sting in its tail. After the 14th, which needs a lofty shot from the tee and ends in a tiered green, come four terrifying holes, of which three are par 5s. At the 15th you must have a sniper's accuracy to stay on the fairway with the drive and make a second shot to carry a ditch and on to a superbly guarded green –

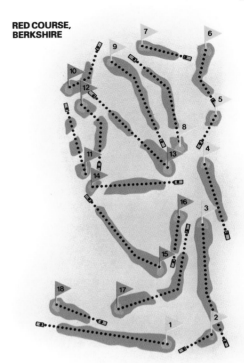

RED COURSE, BERKSHIRE

that is a mere 480-yard par 5. Some may welcome the 16th's 380-yard length par 4 to regain confidence, but the tee is extemely close to the trees and a bunker to the green's right limits access from that direction.

It is the 17th that will demand much of your remaining energy – all 571 yards of it. Arnold Palmer himself quails before its majestic length and wicked dogleg to the left, pulling players into the out of bounds – only the fortuitous visitor can hope for the par 5 here. The course tacks the other way for the final hole. The drive must be played somewhat to the left of centre on the fairway – anything to the right is blocked by a belt of trees. Your second shot has to carry a sudden dip followed by a ditch and

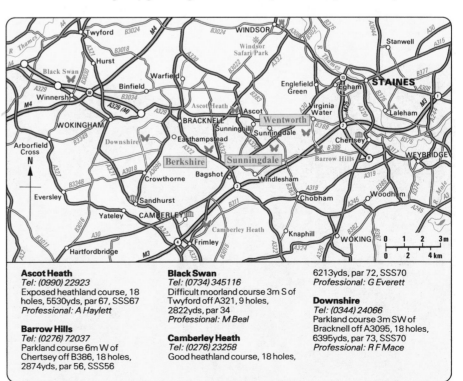

**Ascot Heath**
*Tel: (0990) 22923*
Exposed heathland course, 18 holes, 5530yds, par 67, SSS67
*Professional: A Haylett*

**Barrow Hills**
*Tel: (0276) 72037*
Parkland course 6m W of Chertsey off B386, 18 holes, 2874yds, par 56, SSS56

**Black Swan**
*Tel: (0734) 345116*
Difficult moorland course 3m S of Twyford off A321, 9 holes, 2822yds, par 34
*Professional: M Beal*

**Camberley Heath**
*Tel: (0276) 23258*
Good heathland course, 18 holes,

6213yds, par 72, SSS70
*Professional: G Everett*

**Downshire**
*Tel: (0344) 24066*
Parkland course 3m SW of Bracknell off A3095, 18 holes, 6395yds, par 73, SSS70
*Professional: R F Mace*

**WEST COURSE, WENTWORTH**

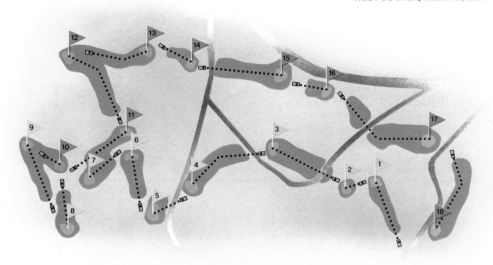

survivors need to play a very well-placed third shot to find the green.

You will, of course, be elevated by the knowledge that you follow in the footsteps of the world's greatest-ever players. Palmer, Nicklaus and Player have all tasted success at Wentworth in the World Matchplay Championship. Gary Player has taken five victories out of the six final appearances he has made here since 1964 and he certainly plays Wentworth with style. Deep in the trees of the so-called 'easy' par 5 of the 4th after an uncharacteristic hook he took one stroke out, made the green in another and then holed a putt from a tree's length away for a birdie. How did the Burma Road get its name? One story is that a large local army population returned from the war and found this tree-lined hell far worse than anything captivity had thrown at them!

These courses are jewels in a stockbroker belt, where massive houses are hidden from view behind high walls and wide gates. They have the very best of neighbours just a few miles away at Windsor. This enchanting spot on the River Thames demands at least one

day's exploration for non-playing members of the family. The town is geared to its royal connections and always thronged with tourists from all parts of the globe. Dominating the neat streets and 17th- and 18th-century buildings is the castle itself – the largest inhabited castle in the world. The State Apartments – open when the Queen is not in residence – date from Edward III's reign and include Queen Mary's Doll's House.

There is plenty to interest the historian, but many are drawn to the open spaces of the Great Park and 300 acres of fragrant rhododendrons, camelias and magnolias in the Valley Gardens. Events are held throughout the summer – the Royal Windsor Horse Show in May, the Windsor Dog Show in June, the Rose and Horticultural Show in July and the Windsor Festival in September/October.

Another 'must' is the Safari Park and Seaworld. Drive through the grounds (with the windows closed) and you will see giraffes, lions, and cheetahs at close quarters and performing dolphins and killer whale shows at the pool complex. Also, at Chessington, there is a

zoo where the exotic inhabitants include gorillas and orang-utans.

On a sunny day the Thames is as congested as Windsor, for there are boats and punts for hire as well as pleasure craft crowded with film-shooting tourists. Further downstream is another royal palace – that of Henry VIII at Hampton Court. The rooms are immaculately preserved, although children might prefer the thrill of losing themselves in the famous Maze.

The Royal Botanical Gardens at Kew are a perfumed and relaxing sanctuary after a day's sightseeing. Green acres flourish with trees, flowers and greenhouses stocked with rare species. Even here there is a palace – built by George III. You can walk from Kew to Hampton Court by simply following the river. An unbroken towpath hugs every meander for a distance of ten miles.

In this place of kings, it is surprising that the county club was never called The Royal Berkshire. Legend has it that the Prince of Wales (later Duke of Windsor) did play a round here. His mistake was that his choice of companion was a professional. He was refused admission for lunch, stormed home to Fort Belvedere and withheld any hope the club might have had of gaining its regal title.

**Angling**
Hurst: Dinton Pastures: fly fishing for fair-sized rainbow trout Apr–Nov
Daily tickets: Dinton Pastures Trout Fishery, Davis Street, Hurst, Twyford
*Tel: (0734) 345480*
Water Authority: as River Mole

River Mole: mainly coarse fishing with some trout chances
Daily tickets: Walton-on-Thames Angling Society (A C Wyatt), 12 River Mead Close, New Haw, Weybridge
*Tel: (0932) 45097*
Water Authority: TWA, 2nd Floor, Reading Bridge House, Reading
*Tel: (0734) 593333*

**Camping**
Laleham: Laleham Park Caravan Site ►►
*Tel: (0784) 54162*
Quiet 150-pitch site (15 caravans) 2m S of Staines
Open Apr–Sep, must book for caravans (& tents Jul–Aug)

**Walking Trails**
Nine Mile Ride: numerous woodland walks off Roman road S of Wokingham

**General**
Camberley: Camberley Museum: local history, costume & archaeology
Open all year Tue–Sat afternoons only
*Tel: (0276) 64483*

National Army Museum, Sandhurst: collections from Indian Army & Irish regiments
Open 10–5 by appointment
*Tel: (0276) 63344 ext 485*
Chertsey: Chertsey Museum: late Georgian mansion housing costume, silver & local history exhibits
Open all year times vary
*Tel: (093 28) 65764*
Chessington: Chessington Zoo: extensive 65-acre complex including children's zoo, bird garden, model railway, circus
Open all year 10–5 (until 7 in summer)
*Tel: (037 27) 27227*
Esher: Claremont: grandiose 18th-century house
Open Feb–Nov first Sat & second Sun in month 2–4.30
*Tel: (0372) 67841*
Windsor: Windsor Castle: restored Norman royal residence (Precincts) open daily
Windsor Safari Park & Seaworld: drive-through zoo, plus marine complex, children's farmyard, picnic areas
Open Apr–mid-Dec daily 10–7 (or dusk)
*Tel: (075 35) 69841*
Wisley: Wisley Gardens: renowned horticultural centre
Open all year 10–7 (or dusk)
*Tel: (048 643) 2234/2235*

# Royal Porthcawl

Royal Porthcawl, Porthcawl, Mid-Glamorgan
*Tel: Porthcawl (065 671) 2251*

To east of town through Nottage

Untypical links course: 6605yds, SSS74

Visitors welcome with reservation
*Professional:* Graham Poor

Hotels: Fairways★★ Porthcawl
*Tel: Porthcawl (065 673) 2085*
(24 rm)

Rose & Crown★ Nottage
*Tel: Porthcawl (065 671) 4850*
(8 rm)

A leading resort of the South Wales coast, Porthcawl owes its popularity to its equidistance between the major port and industrial centres of Cardiff and Swansea. It was to this, then developing, town that a group of Cardiff businessmen came in 1891 seeking permission to play golf. The place they had selected was a cliff-top recreation area called Locks Common to the west of the town on which activities were controlled by the parish council. Within six months the founders had brought in a professional from Westward Ho!, across the Bristol Channel, to lay out nine holes and this premier Welsh links club was well on its way to future fame.

In fact the club grew so fast that Locks Common became totally inadequate and the committee began to look for ways to expand. Below Locks Common the ground ran down to a sand and pebble shore in Rest Bay – another nine holes were added on this land in 1895. The Common was finally abandoned in 1898 when a full eighteen holes were laid out on the foreshore land in a shape that has subsequently been changed very little by the administrations of James Braid, Harry Colt and Tom Simpson who have all added their touches to it in the years prior to World War II.

Every hole at Royal Porthcawl has a view of the sea (the Royal was added to the club's title in 1909) and on a fine day the dark blotch of Exmoor punctuates the horizon across the Bristol Channel. It is also a course on which the wind, battering up this great open stretch of water, can wreak havoc with scores, perhaps no more so than on the exposed lengths of the first three holes which run almost parallel to the shore. At par 4 each, they share the distinct possibility of a hook on to the pebbles of the beach. Both the second and third stray dangerously close to this natural hazard.

You turn away from the sea on the 197-yard par 3 4th hole, where attention is often required to keep off the boundary wall, and sneak into the ring of bunkers guarding the green, with its vicious slope an unexpected final irony to the visitor. The course is now making rising strides uphill to the top plateau, dotted with gorse and heather roughs, via the challenging 485-yard double dogleg of the par 5 5th and the comfortable par 4 6th (the wind can here turn into a blessing).

The only hole that is slightly secluded is the kidney green of the 7th, innocuous looking at 116 yards for a par 3, but a hole that can be like a needle in a haystack to find at times.

The gorse really intrudes on the 8th, with its intimidating blind drive over the heads of the pretty yellow flower haze which makes it a worthy par 5 for its 480-yard length. Holes nine and ten take the player somewhat downhill again, the 9th having a particularly unpleasant slope to the green and the 10th having some playful guard bunkers. Named by local tradition 'Sahara', the 12th is played over a daunting wasteland of shrubs and rough, including a nasty cross-bunker as you head towards the old ground of Locks Common.

Royal Porthcawl finishes on four of the toughest holes on any course – three par 4s and a par 5. This 508-yard 17th hole is a zig-zag with another of the club's Machiavellian blind drives, liberal use of cross-bunkers and terrain like the switch-back in the resort's fun-fair. This frequently brings your face to the wind for the drive over the 18th on the club's east boundary, with another fence to catch the left hooker and terrain to bamboozle the most careful of shots. A famous international golfer came down this par 4 slope to the sea with two full wood shots and a punched seven iron into the wind to get a five and return a card of 86.

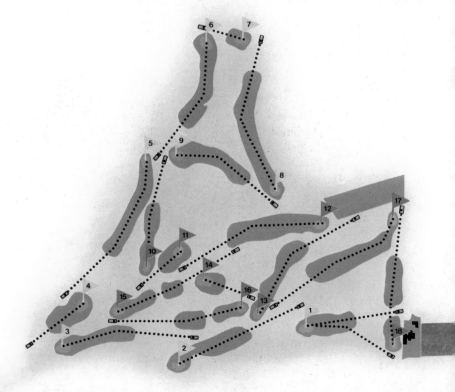

*Work and play near Neath*

He was delighted to take the scratch prize at 14 over par and afterwards named Royal Porthcawl among his ten favourite courses, the other nine of which he could not remember!

The effect the wind has on play here is renowned. Percy Alliss (father of today's celebrity) won a 1932 tournament with an aggregate of 278 including one round of 65 – in the same event the following year John Burton took 14 strokes more to take the prize. Other memorable events here include the 1951 Amateur championship displaying the might of British and US Walker Cup teams and the antics, on and off course, of Bob Hope and Donald Peers. In this event a wholly partisan Welsh crowd cheered local hero Albert Evans into an unexpected semi-final slot, chairing him to the clubhouse. Next day he went under to Charles Coe who was finally vanquished by fellow American Richard Chapman. It was here, too, that the great Curtis Cup duel between Marley Spearman and Jo Anne Gunderson took place in 1964. Both players went round in 71, halved the game and collapsed into each other's arms on the final green with hardly a dry eye among the spectators.

Porthcawl is the playground of industrial South Wales and its entertainments and attractions match those of any other large and popular resort. The harbour, flanked by guest houses, hotels and shops, was once a busy coalport which declined through competition by larger ports such as Barry. Today the harbour is bright with a flotilla of pleasure steamers and private craft, for of all the sports facilities available, power boating and water ski-ing are the most popular.

To the east and west of the town stretch miles of safe-bathing beaches and dunes, although currents can be fast-flowing round the headlands. A miniature railway runs alongside the Eastern promenade to the Coney Beach Amusement Park (modelled on and

named after Coney Island, New York), and the Grand Pavilion stages dances, plays and shows.

On a clear day the tors of Exmoor are just visible across the Bristol Channel from Porthcawl, but closer-by, to the north, are the ruins of the township and castle of Kenfig which was buried by the sands in 1400. (Some say that the bells of Kenfig church can still be heard tolling beneath the water.)

Margam is perhaps best known for its steelworks which extend over four and a half miles and have five blast furnaces, and secondly for Margam Castle. Although the Tudor-Gothic building was damaged by fire, it is the grounds that are worth a visit. A Park Centre has picnic spots, gardens a deer park and heronry. Margam Abbey Museum houses a collection of inscribed and sculptured stones, including a Roman milestone from Port Talbot.

Margam Park is at one end of the Coed Morgannwy Way long distance footpath. A challenge to the energetic walker, it leads over high moor and the forests of Cymer and Margam for twenty-five miles to Craig-y-Llyn. About halfway along the path is the Afan Argoed Countryside Centre with an imaginative Welsh Miners Museum. By entering a simulated coal face and inspecting the kind of equipment used to quarry coal, the visitor gets an explicit impression of the harshness of the job. The ground above is laced with trails.

South Wales is a region of stark contrasts and perhaps because of its intensely industrial background, the open air sports facilities, like the Royal Porthcawl course, are excellent.

**Neath**
Tel: (0639) 3615
Hilly course with natural hazards, 18 holes, 6419yds, par 72, SSS72
*Professional: E Bennett*

**Pyle & Kenfig**
Tel: (065 671) 3093
Breezy downland course 3m N of

Porthcawl off B4283, 18 holes, 6655yds, par 71, SSS72
*Professional: R Thomas*

**Rhondda**
Tel: (0443) 3204
Scenic hilly course, 18 holes, 6241yds, par 70, SSS70
*Professional: C Llewellyn*

**Southerndown**
Tel: (0656) 80326
Downland course near the sea 2m SW of Bridgend off A48, 18 holes, 6615yds, par 70, SSS73
*Professional: H Gould*

**Angling**
Eglwys Nunydd: very good trout reservoir Daily tickets (riparian owner): BSC Sports & Social Club, Groes *Tel: (0792) 781690* Water Authority: as River Garw
River Garw: fair salmon & trout runs in late summer Daily tickets: F D Smiles, 3 Sweet Wells, Pontyrhyl, Pont-y-Cymmer Water Authority: WNWDA, Cambrian Way, Brecon *Tel: (0874) 3181* River Kenfig: minor trout stream Daily tickets: as River Garw Water Authority: as River Garw Porthcawl: harbour boat fishing for thornback, cod & plaice. Lugworm from Trecco Bay Tackle shop: G S Jackson, 14 Well Street, Porthcawl *Tel: (065 671) 2511*

**Camping**
Porthcawl: Broadawell Campsite▶ *Tel: (065 671) 3231* Grassy 85-pitch site (25 caravans) Open Apr–Aug

**General**
Bridgend: Newcastle: ruins of

Norman (and later) stronghold Open all year
Coity: Coity Castle: 12th–16th-century fortress with 3-storeyed tower, 2m NE of Bridgend Open all year
Cymmer: Welsh Miners Museum & Afan Argoed Country Park: interesting museum with simulated coal-face – plus parkland walks Open Easter–Sep (weekends only in winter) *Tel: (063 983) 7175*
Ogmore: Ogmore Castle: 12th-century stone keep within dry moat, 7m W of Maesteg off A4061 Open all year
Port Talbot: Margam Country Park: 840 acres of gardens, picturesque buildings & ruins, plus signposted walks – 4m SE of Port Talbot off A48 Open all year *Tel: (063 96) 87626*
Rhoose: Welsh Aircraft Museum: modern museum housing over 20 aircraft, 4m W of Barry Open all year *Tel: (0222) 29880/562780*

# St Pierre Golf and Country Club

St Pierre Park, Chepstow, Gwent
*Tel: Chepstow (029 12) 5261*

Tree-studded park and meadow courses:
Championship Course: 6660yds, SSS72
New Course: 5194yds, SSS69

Visitors welcome, reservation advisable
*Professional: A Pickles*

Hotels: Beaufort★★ Chepstow
*Tel: Chepstow (029 12) 5074*
(12 rm)

George★★ Chepstow
*Tel: Chepstow (029 12) 2365*
(20 rm)

Portwall★★ Chepstow
*Tel: Chepstow (029 12) 2050*
(15 rm)

Two Rivers★★★ Chepstow
*Tel: Chepstow (029 12) 5151*
(27 rm)

Until 1960, keen golfers in the old market town of Chepstow which tumbles down into the gorge of the River Wye's exit to the Severn, had to be a pretty itinerant group. There was no decent golf course for miles and a trek to Newport or Bristol, across the great expanse of the Severn mouth, was a must. Land simply did not appear to be available in the area. Then came Bill Graham with his dream of a great golf course at this southern end of the Welsh border country – a course to match the delights of the Wye's scenic splendour and the fascination of the nearby ancient Forest of Dean.

The dream came true and its substance is the St Pierre Golf and Country Club, a beautiful parkland course laid out within the tree-studded bounds of an old deer park on the main A48 Chepstow to Newport road. In the middle of the deer park was a house that was getting old in Norman times. It was one of the great historical houses of Monmouthshire and the seat of the St Pierre family, Normans who settled there shortly after the Conquest. At the time of Agincourt, in 1415, the Crown Jewels were cached in the small tower which even now commands the entrance to the inner courtyard of the club's buildings.

In ten quick years golf was developed on the 200-acre park, one of the first new courses to be built in the current golf boom. It is a course of such a quality that major events have been attracted here from the beginning. A frequent venue for the Dunlop Masters Tournament, the latest tribute to the fruition of Graham's plans has been the staging there of the women's international match against America in the Curtis Cup series.

St Pierre has attracted the television cameras, too. If ever there was a natural grandstand, it is the 18th hole at St Pierre. Short

though it is, it crosses the corner of the park's ten-acre lake and comes to a green which has a boundary wall on the left, rough on the right and more bunkers than the Maginot line. This natural arena lies immediately in front of the mansion and the magnificent clubhouse – the perfect setting for the high drama that can accompany the last strokes of any tournament. This is the kind of hole that has professionals reaching for woods on the tee and it is a hole Tony Jacklin has every reason to remember. Here he took the Masters title with a fearless three wood shot that came incredibly within a yard of the hole.

This championship Old Course is the work of golf architect Ken Cotton, and with the estate's many assets he must have found it one of his easier tasks. The very mature trees spaced over the park and meadow turf are the major obstacle to amateur and professional alike on this testing 6619-yard course.

The opening holes are played between daunting ranks of chestnuts which have the visitors believing they move to block every shot. The ground rises to a short hole on the top of an escarpment from which it is possible to see the foothills of the Brecon Beacons or turn and gaze across the Severn to the coast of the West Country. The many long par 5 holes on the course make it very difficult indeed to play to handicap. Fainter hearts will try the predominantly meadowland delights of the so-called New Course designed by Bill Cox.

Bill Graham's final achievement was to achieve a membership list of 1 400 keen golfers within three years of opening. Even if the golf does not appeal, the club's fine facilities, which include accommodation for up to 110 people, are among the best in Britain.

The catchment area is much larger than meets the eye, for Chepstow is on the doorstep of the Forest of Dean, a ride across the Severn bridge away from Bristol via the M4, and an

easy drive from Gloucester and the major towns of South Wales.

In exploring Chepstow's environs, it is easy to become dizzy and confused as to which

**Angling**
Llandegfedd Reservoir: huge stillwater offering fly fishing for trout
Daily tickets: on-site ticket machine
Water Authority: as River Wye
Newport: beach fishing for bass, sole, pouting plus seasonal cod
Tackle shop: Arc Fishing Tackle, 60 Caerleon Road, Newport
*Tel: (0633) 215785*
River Wye: renowned salmon fishing
Daily tickets (for Llandogo or Tintern): J Jones, The Rock, Tintern
Water Authority: WNWDA, Cambrian Way, Brecon
*Tel: (0874) 3181*

**Camping**
Chepstow: Trax Campsite►►
Level 75-pitch site by estuary
Open Apr–Sep, no bookings
Mitchel Troy: Glen Trothy Caravan & Camping Site►►
*Tel: (0600) 2295*
Level 76-pitch site near river
Open Apr–Oct must book public holidays

**General**
Caerleon: Amphitheatre: excavated Roman stadium 2m NE of

Newport off A449
Open all year
Caldicot: Caldicot Castle, Museum & Countryside Park: Norman castle, local history museum & large grounds
Open Mar–Oct (ex Sat) park open all year
*Tel: (0291) 420241*
Chapel Hill: Tintern Abbey: extensive remains of 13th-century Cistercian church, 5m N of Chepstow off A466
Open all year
Chepstow: Chepstow Castle: 11th-century masonry fortress, a Civil War garrison
Open all year
Clearwell: Clearwell Caves & Ancient Iron Mines: local mining & geological site with picnic area
Open Easter–Sep (ex Mon & Sat)
*Tel: (0594) 23700* for off-season party booking
Penhow: Penhow Castle: 12th-century fortress, the oldest still inhabited in Wales
Open Easter–Sep daily 10–6 (ex Mon & Tue)
*Tel: (0633) 400800*
Wolvesnewton: Wolvesnewton Folk Museum & Craft Centre: 18th-century barn housing agricultural, craft & toy collections, 12m NW of Chepstow off B4235

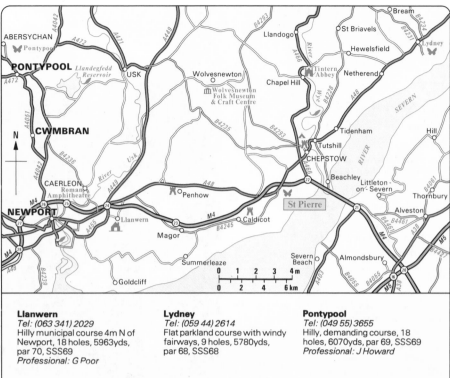

country you are in. Chepstow itself has a schizoid history, decreed English at one time, and now Welsh. The castle, ruined but open to the public, was a Royalist stronghold and the museum outlines the town's history of the once-important shipbuilding and salmon fishery industries. Follow the steep streets round a one-way system and across the Wye and you return to Gloucestershire and head off the A48 which skirts the Severn to the ancient Forest of Dean.

Lying 'in the eye of the Severn and the Wye' it is an enchanting area of rounded hills, broadleaf and coniferous forest and tiny villages where sheep graze freely by the roadside. Numerous forest trails exist and the Forestry Commission publishes informative leaflets pointing out to ramblers the likely haunts of deer, squirrels and badgers.

Iron mines, like those at Clearwell Caves, were worked for 3000 years until as recently as 1945. Visitors can go inside to see a collection of geological samples and mining equipment before taking refreshment at Clearwell Castle. This mock-Gothic building is bordered by formal gardens and a Bird Park. Railway enthusiasts will demand spending a morning at the Norchard Steam Centre. There is a collection of rolling stock, old and new, to wonder at, and steam days (mostly in August) throughout the summer, when one of the mighty steam engines chugs along about a mile of track into the forest depths.

The slow-flowing waters of the Wye can be followed upstream along the A466 (in Wales). Although it has produced record-breaking catches of salmon, the Wye can be a frustrating river to fish. Much of it is privately owned and rods are expensive; even coarse fishing is governed by strict regulations in many sections. Canoeists have more freedom with launching points at Saracen's Head, Symonds Yat and Huntsham Bridge, but launching is forbidden

here because this is Forestry Commission land.

If you simply want to view the splendour of the river, the best spot of many is Symonds Yat. Here, from tables scattered under oak and beech trees, picnickers look out across a mighty sweep of the Wye before it is funnelled into a narrow gorge. A trail follows the cliff-top, with views of the river, for almost three miles.

Edging the Forest of Dean to the east is the long estuary of the River Severn. Its watery phenomenon, the Severn Bore, is a frequent sight from the A48, but it reaches its greatest height on only about twenty-five days of the year (a Heart of England Tourist Board free

information sheet gives dates for better-than-usual sightings).

To the west of the Wye is the Land of Song; the bustling towns of Newport and Cardiff, the salmon-stocked waters of the Usk and fine walking country in the foothills of the formidable Black Mountains.

Thanks to vastly improved road schemes, Chepstow can claim to be not only the gateway to Wales, but to a much larger region of outstanding countryside. Whether you are encountering the area or the course of St Pierre for the first time, the memory of the Wye from Symonds Yat is bound to bring you back again.

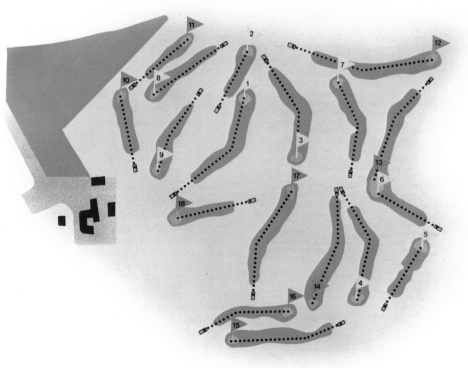

# Royal St David's

Royal St David's, Harlech,
Gwynedd
*Tel: Harlech (0766) 780203*

On A496 just outside town

Windy links close to extensive sands:
6495yds, SSS72

Visitors welcome all week
*Professional: John Barnett*

Hotels: Cae Nest Hall★ Llanbedr
*Tel: Barmouth (034 123) 349*

St Davids★★ Harlech
*Tel: Harlech (0766) 78036*
(80 rm)

Take a combination of history, mountain views, bracing sea breezes and most golfers would prick up their ears – add to that the promise of a first-class game on championship-standard links and holiday plans will be laid. This is Harlech, home of the Royal St David's club and among the principal foci of golf in Wales. For under the stern gaze of Harlech's mighty castle, one of the ring of fortifications built by Edward I to get a grip on the unruly Welsh hill tribes, is a links course with a

### Angling
River Artro: good bass in estuary, fair access for visitors
Daily tickets: The Post Office, Llanbedr
*Tel: (034 123) 201*
Water Authority: WNWDA, Cambrian Way, Brecon
*Tel: (0874) 3181*
Trawsfynydd Lake: large, regularly re-stocked trout reservoir
Daily tickets: H K & P A Lewis, Trawsfynydd
*Tel: (076 687) 234*
Water Authority: as River Artro
Porthmadog: Traeth Bach estuary for bass, flounder, plaice. Boat fishing for most flatfish
Tackle shop: The Angling Centre, 11 High Street, Porthmadog
*Tel: (0766) 2464*

### Camping
Penrhyndeudraeth: Bwlch Bryn Caravan Park ▶
*Tel: (0766) 770365*
Sloping 10-pitch site (no tents)
Open Mar–Oct, must book Jul–Aug
Porthmadog: Tyddyn Llwyn Caravan Site ▶
*Tel: (0766) 2205*
237-pitch upland site (7 caravans)
Open Mar–Oct, must book Jul–Aug
Tal-y-Bont: Islaw R'ffordd Caravan Site ▶▶▶

*Tel: (034 17) 269*
425-pitch (25 caravans) meadowland site 4m N of Barmouth
Open Easter–Oct, no bookings

### Walking Trails
Snowdonia: 838 square miles woodland, mountains & parkland. For further information:
Gwyddfor House, High Street, Harlech
*Tel: (076673) 658*

### General
Dolgellau: Cymmer Abbey: remains of 13th-century monastery
Open all year
Harlech: Harlech Castle: fine 13th-century fortress with imposing gatehouse
Open all year
Old Llanfair Slate Quarries: guided tours through man-made caverns
Open Easter–mid-Oct daily 10–5.30
*Tel: (076 673) 247*
Portmeirion: fantasy village 2m SE of Porthmadog, scene of TV's *The Prisoner*
Open Mar–Nov daily
*Tel: (0766) 770228*
Porthmadog: Festiniog Railway: historic narrow-gauge railway re-opened by steam enthusiasts
Daily service Mar–Nov
*Tel: (0766) 2384*

stunning range of attractions for the visitor.

Lying next to Morfa Harlech sands, which once featured as those of the Sahara for the film 'Brides of Fu Manchu', Royal St David's lands have mountains on the doorstep which you can almost reach out and touch. Sand dunes capped by tall rush grass divide and protect the course from the sea, creating ideal golf conditions that were first realised by a group of landed and affluent gentlemen lead by the Hon Harold Finch-Hatton and W H More, then Crown Agent for Wales, in 1894.

With the proximity of the Snowdonia National Park, one might expect to encounter some outcrops of rock and heath on the course but the original architects stuck to the flat of the foreshore, letting the holes lie naturally on the many existing hazard possibilities and undulations left by thousands of years' pounding by the Irish Sea across Cardigan Bay.

Harlech begins with a drive away from the castle along an undulating fairway with a close entry to the green and some midway traps set to catch the slice. It is wise to note that there is very little wind shelter at Harlech and the gusts from the sea can demolish your game. A 2nd of

373 yards is played in the opposite direction to reach the first of the holes with a bite to it.

With gorse to the left and a track to the right, the 463-yard par 4 makes a straight drive essential to get to the green, guarded by sand to the left, right and centre. First of Harlech's short holes, a 4th of 188 yards has a dip in front of the raised green which makes distance judgement interesting. On the same level is the tee of the 5th on which a good drive to carry the cross bunkers is rewarded by a better opening to the green.

Watch the under-clubbed second shot on the 6th as there is a trap set for it, but generally players should be up on the card in fettle to tackle the first par 5 of 481 yards at the 7th. Turning slightly left, this hole is often played against the prevailing wind – a set of four bunkers straddle the fairway and the entry to the plateau green demands a resolute shot over traps at the front.

There is a distinct similarity between the 9th and the 4th in that it is played crosswind to a tight green which rises from the front. Again the risk is to under-club. Six of the next seven holes are played along the sea boundary, with much more use being made of the interesting natural dune formations.

This is particularly noticeable on the short 11th, a 144-yard hole running between two high banks making it an ideal arena for spectators. The banks funnel together towards the green entrance which is over an enormous expanse of cross bunker. On the long dogleg of the 12th, a drive to the left is the way to open up the shot to the green but hookers run the risk of a line of bunkers streamed down its 437-yard length. The tee is high. Much the same applies to the 13th, except that the traps are ranged right and interspersed by roughs of hardy sea rushes.

Bemusing length at 218 yards makes the blind 14th a short hole to be reckoned with and another of Harlech's softeners for a test in store. Here, on the slight dogleg of the 15th, the last of the sea holes, you drive over rough along a fairway lined by dunes that narrow down to a tantalising second shot on to a sunken green.

There have been plans to modify Harlech's final holes, which have not as yet come to fruition. It comes as a shock to realise on the 16th tee that you have played the best part of a round within a couple of drives of Cardigan Bay and this is the first glimpse of it. Since the plan for change involves re-designing the great 17th hole, it is small wonder that little has happened. This is a 427-yard par 4 along an undulating fairway on which the cautious play well short to avoid the huge bunker in front of the green. Harlech's final hole is something of an anti-climax being a 202-yard par 3, often downwind to a richly-bunkered green.

Royal St David's was indeed royal. Edward VII gave the club his patronage and the Duke of Windsor (Edward VIII), while Prince of Wales, captained the club in 1935. Harlech has staged all the major events of the Welsh

calendar and in 1960 and 1967 this club was the venue for the Curtis Cup.

Look for stimulus off the course and you will not be disappointed. This ranges from seaside sun spots, offshore fishing and historical interest to the splendours of Snowdonia. No wonder the Men of Harlech had something to sing about! (They did, in fact, hold the rugged castle which dominates Harlech for eight years against the Yorkists during the Wars of the Roses.) Whether because of the song or the breathtaking views across Tremadoc Bay to the Lleyn peninsula, Harlech Castle draws thousands of photo-snapping tourists each year; luckily, the magnificent countryside offers an escape in high season.

Two nature trails a few miles to the south are Cwm Nantcol and Cefn Isa at Salem Chapel, Llanbedr (half a mile and two miles long respectively); but the more serious walker can tackle a ten-mile hike along Roman Steps – a donkey track which crosses a saddle of the dramatic Rhinog Mountains to the beautiful valley of the River Eden.

To the north is the fantasy architectural village of Portmeirion created by Clough Williams-Ellis. Set on the shores of Cardigan

Bay amid sub-tropical woodland, are an unlikely mixture of styles, from Jacobean to Oriental. Nearby, Gwylt Gardens in early summer are heavy with the scent of rhododendrons and azaleas are ablaze with their colours.

Criccieth has hardly changed since Victoria's reign; a quiet, crescent-shaped beach with a 13th-century castle and views of Snowdonia – and famous locally for its ice-cream. Nearby Llanystumdwy was the home of Wales' most celebrated politician, Lloyd George. It is where he chose to be buried. A museum near his grave, on the banks of the River Dwyfor, documents his distinguished career in photographs and momentoes.

Even enthusiastic golfers have been tempted away from their game by the appeal of the Festiniog Railway, which chugs between Blaenau Ffestiniog to the sea at Porthmadog. The promise of a catch of bass, dab or plaice at Morfa Bychan will mean more to some than the view of Cnicht, the Matterhorn of Wales, which rises as a backdrop to Porthmadog's harbour and sea wall (the Cob).

Such a combination makes a memorable holiday, and campers and caravanners have several sites from which to choose a base.

**Ffestiniog**
Moorland course within Snowdonia, 9 holes, 4944yds, par 68, SSS64

**Porthmadog**
Tel: (0766) 2037
Links course with good views, 18 holes, 5600yds, par 68, SSS67
Professional: P Bright

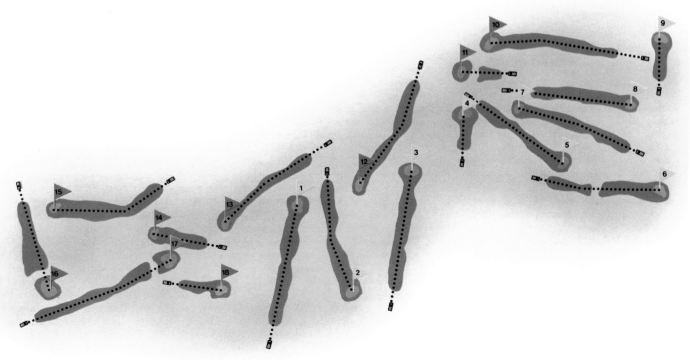

# Caernarvonshire and North Wales

Caernarvonshire (Conwy),
The Morfa, Conwy, Gwynedd
*Tel: Conwy (049 263) 2423*

North Wales, 72 Brynian Road,
West Shore, Llandudno, Clwyd
*Tel: Llandudno (0492) 75325*

Caernarvonshire

Take coast road A55, out of town ¾ mile on right

Classic links course: 6664yds, SSS73

Visitors welcome with club introduction
*Professional:* Peter Lees

North Wales

Between A496 and sea on west edge of town

Pretty links course: 6132yds, SSS69

Visitors welcome with club introduction
*Professional:* Ceri Cousins

Hotels: Bryn Cregin★★ Deganwy
*Tel: Llandudno (0492) 83402*
(24 rm)

Castle★★ Conwy
*Tel: Conwy (049 263) 2324*
(28 rm)

Clarence★★ Llandudno
*Tel: Llandudno (0492) 786485*
(74 rm)

Deganwy Castle★★ Deganwy
*Tel: Llandudno (0492) 83358*
(33 rm)

Empire★★★ Llandudno
*Tel: (0492) 77260*
(51 rm)

Gogarth Abbey★★★ Llandudno
*Tel: Llandudno (0492) 76212*

Within half an hour's drive of the majestic peaks of Snowdonia's highest range, Yr Wydd-fa itself, are the major North Wales coast resorts of Llandudno and Colwyn Bay. They occupy the narrow strip of land which is all that is left of Wales as the mountains tumble to the sea and offer all the fun of the fair against a backdrop of dramatic purple peaks and ridges, open foothills and mountain streams which are the tributaries of the Conwy River. At the mouth of the river, barely a couple of miles from the well-preserved Telford suspension bridge which once funnelled coast traffic into Conwy town, are two splendid golf courses, one each side of the river. Facing each other, north-south across Conwy Sands, are the Caernarvonshire Club, which is just outside Conwy and the North Wales Club on the western edge of Llandudno. Founded in 1889,

the Caernarvonshire lies on natural links land of sandhills and sea rushes, speckled with gorse and overlaid by fine old sea turf.

The land overlooks the estuary of the Conwy in which many of the Mulberry harbour sections for the D-Day landings were built. To the east is the pretty village of Deganwy and in the distance, to the north is the smudge of Llandudno resting between the two humps of the Great and Little Ormes. On the western horizon is the dark line of Anglesey across the Menai Straits, punctuated by the dot of the bird sanctuary, Puffin Island.

Conwy's course begins on a wide fairway with impending trouble to the right for the slicer and an interesting second shot played over a ridge through two large bunkers on to a sunken green. Crosswinds add to the difficulty of the 2nd, a par 3 of 152 yards, with an out of bounds marked by an old wall to the right. The green is tiered slightly into the face of a belligerently bunkered sandhill. On the 3rd, players meet the principal Conwy hazard of gorse, along a hole parallel with the shore. The drive must have a good carry to overstep the gorse from the tee, leaving the rest of the 331 yards to a pitch on to the plateau green.

Driving back from the sea towards the distant mountains of Snowdonia, the 398-yard 4th needs a careful tee shot to allow an easier second bite to the new green. This demand for accuracy is echoed on the 5th, with a more strenuous 454-yard length. Broad though the fairway may seem, bushes bound the right to catch the slice and there is a rough and tumble of hillocks to the left. Distance of the pitch has to be judged spot-on to find the green. In the background is the promontory of Penmaen-bach. Overcome the 6th's deceptive distance of 191 yards and you are away to the 514 yards par 5 of the 7th, requiring two open-shouldered shots in playing down to a narrowed green entrance.

High above the 7th green and with a grand panorama of all Conwy's many sights, is the 8th tee. Turning from the view you will need all your concentration for this rather undulat-

ing fairway which demands a pin-point second shot to attain the slightly sloping green. The first leg finishes with a good long driving hole over guide posts to a blind green. It is the 10th that brings you back to the clubhouse from the seaward side of the course. A good drive will enable your second shot to clear a ridge on the approach which must be gauged to the right to open up the length of the green.

Gorse is very prolific over most of the holes of the course's second leg and it is to be reckoned with on the 11th hole of 384 yards. Gorse has to be carried from the tee shot and it lines the fairway all the way to a narrow entrance to a well-guarded green. A blind tee shot over a well-sited guide post is the correct line on the 12th, an invigorating par 5 of 512 yards. Beware the funnelling of the green entrance as you play your approach shot. There are more out-of-sight targets on the 13th, a slight dogleg of 396 yards to a green hedged with traps.

Conwy has one of the most searching finishes in Welsh golf, the 15th and 16th holes in particular being the home of gorse, rendering the odd bunker superfluous. A 15th of 404 yards is a dogleg right, requiring a tee shot placed to the left of the fairway to get a good opening on to the green approach. The green is a pretty emerald in a setting of the yellow whins. The pressure is kept up on the 16th, played from a plateau with a slight dogleg left to a bunker-ringed green.

There is the brief respite of the 17th, a 147-yard par 3 of character before tackling the Caernarvonshire's final par 4 of 362 yards. Driving towards the front of the clubhouse, a straight line from the tee is a must to avoid more gorse and a second shot is played over a ridge to a green beset by traps.

In the club's early records is a round of 66 by Scottish professional Alex Herd, to be broken only a year later (1910) by George Duncan's 65. This colourful character became the club's pro until he was dismissed for his frequent absences when he was to be found on the football field. The club has hosted all the Welsh main events, prestigious contests such

*Bodnant Gardens, Conwy Valley*

4s, the first being a left-hand dogleg of 344 yards with an out of bounds to the left. Following on is the 'The Furze', played into the prevailing wind more often than not, and shot as a dogleg to the left to avoid a rough hillock. The family professionals have their marker on the 3rd, 'The Collins', which is now driven down from an elevated tee to a green defined by left and right bunkers.

The North Wales is on land between the railway and the sea (unlike Llandudno's Maesdu course hedged by houses on the opposite side of the line) and the 4th skirts the track boundary. Two spectacular bunkers make the green visible from the tee on this 200-yard hole. A slope for the second shot gives the 5th the tag of 'The Hill'. This is another hole played as a dogleg, avoiding gorse rough on the left. From Bryn Lupus tee is a glorious view of the Isle of Anglesey. Your drive must carry the stream which runs down the right-hand side and across the fairway – a second water hazard bars the green approach.

A railway boundary comes into play for hookers on 'The Dyke', 498 yards, par 5, and the putt is the decider on the hole's undulating green. Following the railway is the 352-yard par 4 of 'Vardre', a blind shot over guide posts to avoid a major patch of rough ground. It is the sea which intimidates on the final hole of the first leg aptly named 'The Chasm' for the ravine that must be carried with the drive from an elevated tee to a green impressively bunkered on the left.

Local golfers aim for the Great Orme off the 10th tee on the homeward run. A 400-yard hole parallel with the sea named 'The Ruins', a long cross bunker intrudes just a 100 yards short of the green, which the visitor should know slopes left to right. It is a fine softener for the severe 11th ('Castell') a par 4 of 420 yards. Sea and gorse mark the left and a water hazard the

right, with undulating rough between tee and fairway. There are ridges on either side of a well-defined green.

After the front to back slope of the 12th green, you must get to grips with 'Hades', a 13th holding all the evil import of its name and number. It is just 182 yards, but played towards the sea to a green set in a two-thirds amphitheatre of whins – the wind takes the ball short from the elevated tee making this just as much power play as a test of accuracy.

At 530 yards, 'The Long' is the North Wales' tiger par 5, taken from an elevated tee allowing a view of the hole all the way to the green. A second shot must be placed to give a comfortable approach through the long left and right green bunkers.

North Wales' unusual finish is 4,3,3,4. The 16th, named a self-explanatory 'OL', is a beautiful seaside short hole played from a banked tee over a bowl of semi-rough. While the 17th, 'LO', is only 100 yards – enough to break many a card. The ground slopes away from the green into the bowl of the previous hole and it is difficult to judge the distance.

Paradise is gained at the 18th, a finisher of

as the Martini International, and several other championship qualifiers. In 1981 the club stages the British Ladies'Open Amateur.

Across the estuary, on the Warren sands of Llandudno, is the rival championship links of the North Wales Club. Formed in 1894, the club's history is dominated by the name of Collins. First professional to the club was Fred Collins who was succeeded by his nephew W Sidney Collins in 1937, a fine golfing teacher who retired as recently as 1979. Honours for creating the course go to the all-round sportsman, T D Cummins, who first leased the rough and tumble of the Warren from the Ecclesiastical Commissioners. Like many Scottish courses, the holes of this club bear names.

The North Wales tees off on three stiff par

**CAERNARVONSHIRE GOLF COURSE**

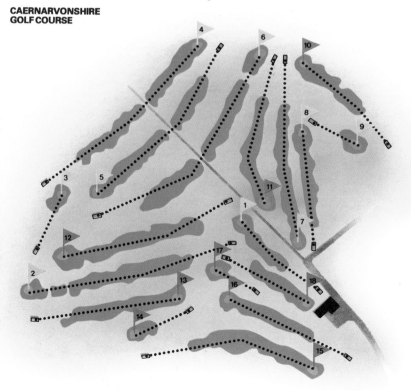

**Angling**
River Conwy: excellent sea trout with good chances for visitors
Daily tickets: Dolgarrog Fishing Club (F A Corrie), 3 Taylor Avenue, Dolgarrog *Tel: (049 269) 651*
Water Authority: WNWDA (Gwynedd Rivers Division), Cambrian Way, Brecon *Tel: (0874) 3181*
Llandudno: fishing from pier & jetty for bass, flounder, pollack. Boat fishing may add dogfish, ray & tope
Tackle shop: Snowdonia Sports, Augusta Street, Llandudno *Tel: (0492) 75442*
River Roe: 8m Conwy tributary Daily tickets: as River Conwy
Water Authority: as River Conwy

**Camping**
Llandudno: Glan Morfa Farm ▶ *Tel: (0492) 81111* Small 20-pitch site (no tents) 2m S of Llandudno Open all year, no bookings
Llysfaen: Westwood Caravan Park ▶ *Tel: (0492) 57410* Smallish 43-pitch site (no tents) 4m E of Colwyn Bay Open Apr–Oct, must book
Penmaenmawr: Gardens Caravan Park ▶▶▶ *Tel: (0492) 622334* Level 12-pitch site (no tents) Open Easter–Sep, must book

**Riding**
Llanfairfechan: Rhiwaiu Riding Centre (Ms R M Hill), Llanfairfechan, Conwy *Tel: (0248) 680094*

**Walking Trails**
Snowdonia: 838 square miles of woodland, mountains & parkland. For further information: Castle Street, Conwy *Tel: (049 263) 2248*

**General**
Colwyn Bay: Welsh Mountain Zoo & Botanic Gardens: large variety of animals & flora Open all year *Tel: (0492) 2938*
Conwy: Conwy Castle: imposing 13th-century fortress Open all year
Plas Mawr: superb 16th-century town house with permanent art exhibition Open all year daily (ex mid-Dec–mid-Jan *Tel: (049 263) 3413*
Smallest House: reputedly smallest dwelling in Britain Open Easter–Oct daily 10–6
Llanrwst: Llanrwst Transport Group Museum: locomotives, wagons, buses & smaller exhibits Open first Sun each month 10–4.30 *Tel: (0492) 82394*
Tal-y-Cafn: Bodnant Garden: fine collection of shrubs & trees 8m N of Llanrwst off A470 Open mid-Mar–Oct daily 10–5 (no dogs or prams)

*Maesdu Golf Course, Llandudno*

305 yards playing away from the sea from a tee with good views. You drive down a gulley to the fairway with gorse and sand dune hazards, with a wicked bunker lying in wait.

North Wales does have its local counter-point in the Maesdu course and the rocky hump of the Great Orme was played over, until the Second World War. Now this guardian of Llandudno's flank is walked over by thousands of tourists every year, many of them ascending to the summit by the rack tramway from the town below. There is also an alpine-style cable car running from close to the town's pier.

Llandudno is Wales' prime seaside attraction. Broad promenades sweep round the bay between the two Ormes with row upon row of Edwardian and Victorian hotels and guest-houses lining the seafront. It has, of course, all the major fun attractions of a family resort including gardens, two miniature golf courses, a nature trail on the Great Orme and the Marine Drive toll road running around the dramatic promontory.

Across the river mouth by the impressive new road bridge is the delightful town of Conwy, a mediaeval fortified borough with a castle which is one of the ring established by Edward I to subdue the Welsh. Morfa Beach, close to the Caernarvonshire Club, is a safe sandy beach for bathing. Boat trips run from the harbour out into the sea and the Menai Straits for spectacular views of Anglesey which include Beaumaris, another of the fortified settlements for which Wales is famed.

Few families will visit this part of Wales without a trip to the mountain fastnesses of Snowdonia. A National Park area of outstand-ing beauty, the summit of Snowdon forms the natural focal point of an area brimming with recreational opportunities. Do not venture on to the hills here without stout footwear and adequate emergency clothing, as the weather can change very suddenly for the worse on the higher slopes. Less energetic walkers will ap-preciate the signed nature trails dotted about the Park and all within easy driving range of the coastal strip. Cwm Idwal in particular is a naturalist's paradise which contains many species of plant unique to this valley. The really lazy way up Snowdon is on the rack railway from Llanberis – one-way tickets would enable you to make the return journey on foot to the village (an easy four-mile trek).

To take in a large slice of the Park in a day would be criminal but the way back from Snowdonia's heart can be a stimulating round tour via Caernarvon, scene of the Prince of Wales' investiture, and the shores of the Menai Straits. This is an area to which fishermen will be drawn, there being good shore marks along the coast road with catches of bass and whiting later in the year. There is boat fishing too.

The whole of the Park and the coastal strip is a campers' paradise, with many sites in the hills catering for climbers, walkers, canoeists and anglers hunting the elusive trout in the many small lakes and rivers of the region.

Of all the courses in this book, worthy of inclusion for their great golfing merit, few have the surroundings and varied family attrac-tions in such great number as the Caernarvon-shire and North Wales on Snowdon's doorstep. This is a place where the visitor is welcomed with open arms for a rewarding long stay that can include every ingredient for enjoyment.

**NORTH WALES GOLF COURSE**

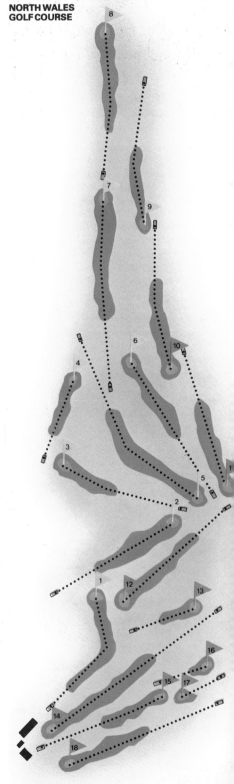

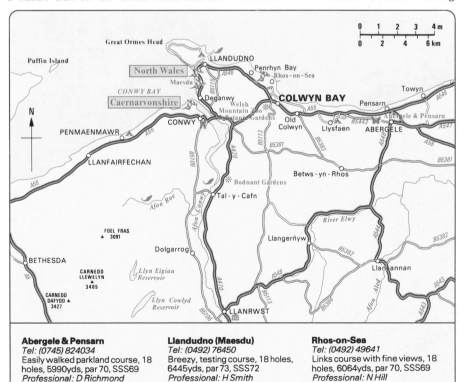

**Abergele & Pensarn**
Tel: (0745) 824034
Easily walked parkland course, 18 holes, 5990yds, par 70, SSS69
*Professional: D Richmond*

**Llandudno (Maesdu)**
Tel: (0492) 76450
Breezy, testing course, 18 holes, 6445yds, par 73, SSS72
*Professional: H Smith*

**Rhos-on-Sea**
Tel: (0492) 49641
Links course with fine views, 18 holes, 6064yds, par 70, SSS69
*Professional: N Hill*

# Fulford

**Fulford, Heslington Lane, York, North Yorkshire**
*Tel: York (0904) 55212*

From York drive 1 mile on A19, signposted to university

Flat parkland and moorland course: 6779yds, SSS72
*Course designer:* Dr MacKenzie

Visitors welcome with club introduction
*Professional:* B Hessay

Hotels: Abbey Park★★★ York
*Tel: York (0904) 25481*
(84 rm)

Royal Station★★★★ York
*Tel: York (0904) 53681*
(130 rm)

White Swan★★ York
*Tel: York (0904) 28851*
(30 rm)

Yorkshire's industrial belt, stretching from the Leeds/Bradford conurbation to its tail in the North Riding capital of York itself, is remarkably well-endowed with golf courses of the highest order. Leeds boasts a cluster of five of the finest tests of golf that can be found in any inland city. Headingley, better known for cricket and rugby league, has a course which is eclipsed by mighty Moortown (scene of the epic 1929 Ryder Cup), beautiful and severe Allwoodley and, just beyond the city limits, Sand Moor with its views over the Harewood estate. That does not include the twenty-seven holes of Moor Allerton, the only example of American designer Robert Trent Jones' work in Britain. Genteel Harrogate has two clubs of championship standard at Pannal and ancient Starbeck. However, it is to Fulford near York, that beautiful cathedral city making a great

touring base, that many holidaying players will turn for a taste of Yorkshire golf at its best.

Fulford Golf Club has become famous in recent years as the home of the Benson & Hedges Golf Festival, but before the first of these events was held there in 1971 the course was the venue for many major amateur events. The Benson & Hedges, staged at Fulford until 1978, returned again in 1980.

For an inland course in a county that has more than its share of ups and downs, it is something of a surprise to find Fulford is quite flat. It is a course dominated by fine copper beech and oak trees, many of which define the shape of the shot both from the tee and to the green. On this superb parkland the good driver is always rewarded. There are two distinctly different sets of holes, one starting from the 1st to the 6th on the way out and the other from the 12th, homeward to the finishing green which is set under the clubhouse. These are joined by a loop from the 7th to the 11th. The design, by Dr Mackenzie, is such that there are no escape routes on to adjoining fairways.

A cinder road marches the length of the first fairway on the left hand side, complementing a set of bunkers and trees on the right which have to be avoided with the tee shot. A mid or a short iron should make the green. The 2nd is one of Fulford's good driving holes – a lot of average drivers will fall foul of the three bunkers placed to the left. A long iron will certainly be needed to get to a green that slopes disturbingly from left to right.

Among the more testing holes is the short 3rd which usually requires a long iron – the green slopes from the back to the front. Anything short stays on the front edge and if the ball takes to the back of the green it is likely to bounce through.

A long out of bounds to the left of the 4th is matched by scrubland on the right but there are no bunkers to contend with from the tee, which should be followed by a long iron to the raised green surrounded by gorse.

The development of a new by-pass that sliced through the course has meant that

players now cross a footbridge to the new 6th, a magnificent par 5 set back in the trees. Very few players will make this green in two. Fulford's 7th used to be no more than a drive and a pitch to a postage stamp green ringed by bunkers. A new tee, the result of the roadworks, has added considerably to the severity of the 7th, which retains the small green.

There is a distinct change of character at the 8th, which has much more of a moorland feel to it. There is gorse and heather to contend with on its dogleg to the left. Many players use an iron here as a safe means of gaining the turn which leaves only a short iron to the green. While being somewhat short for a par 5, the 9th, another left-hand dogleg, is dominated by marshland and heather – heather actually crosses the fairway at one point. As with many Fulford fairways, this one slopes from left to right. Players start their way home with a short hole from an exposed tee which presents problems in club selection. Anything from a medium to short iron may be required if the wind is up. A very large bunker to the left, one of a set guarding this forward sloping green, is the main one to avoid.

It is a big cross-bunker that causes trouble on

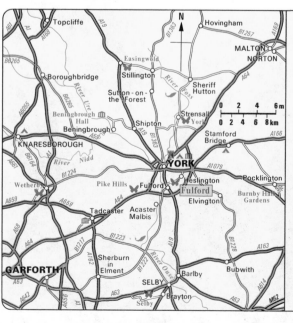

**Easingwold**
*Tel: (0347) 21486*
Pleasant parkland course, 18 holes, 6190yds, par 72, SSS70

**Pike Hills (York)**
*Tel: (0904) 66566*
Parkland course enclosing nature reserve, 18 holes, 5960yds, par 71, SSS69
*Professional: G Love*

**Selby**
*Tel: (075 782) 622*
Flattish links course, 18 holes, 6223yds, par 70, SSS70
*Professional: P Hopper*

**Wetherby**
*Tel: (0937) 2527*
Scenic parkland course 2m N of Wetherby off A1, 18 holes, 6061yds, par 71, SSS69
*Professional: A Hirst*

**York**
*Tel: (0904) 490304*
Interesting parkland course, 18 holes, 6205yds, par 70, SSS71
*Professional: A Howell*

**Angling**
River Foss: coarse fishing for mainly pike
Free fishing
Water Authority: YWA, West Riding House, 67 Albion Street, Leeds
*Tel: (0532) 448201*
River Ouse: fair coarse fishing
Free fishing
Water Authority: as River Foss
York: Tackle shop: Hookes of York Ltd, 28–30 Coppergate, York
*Tel: (0904) 55073*

**Camping**
Knaresborough: Allerton Park Caravan Site ▶▶▶
*Tel: (0901) 30569*
Sloping 30-pitch site (no tents) 4m E of Knaresborough
Open Apr–Oct, must book Bank holidays
Stamford Bridge: Weir Caravan Park ▶▶▶
*Tel: (0759) 71377*
Gently sloping 60-pitch site
Open Apr–Oct, no bookings
York: Caravan Club Site ▶▶
*Tel: (0904) 58997*
Level, grassy 90-pitch site (20 tents)
Open Apr–Sep, must book
Chestnut Farm Caravans ▶▶▶
*Tel: (0904) 706371*
Grassy 25-pitch site (no tents) 4m S of York
Open Apr–Oct, must book public holidays

**Sailing**
Acaster Malbis: access to 15m of deep river, take minor road off A64 4m S of

York. Permission on the spot

**General**
Beningbrough: Beningbrough Hall: 18th-century house in wooded park
Open Apr–Oct daily 12–6
Pocklington: Burnby Hall Gardens & Stewart Collection: lovely lily-pond gardens & museum of sports trophies
Open May–Sep daily (weekends only in winter) – gardens open all year
*Tel: (075 92) 2068/2114*
Tadcaster: The Ark Museum: early timbered house, now pubs & brewing museum
Open all year (Tue, Wed & Thu 2–4)
*Tel: (0937) 833085*
York: City Art Gallery: fine collection of European & British paintings, plus modern pottery
Open all year (Mon–Fri)
*Tel: (0904) 23839*
Guildhall: 15th-century building with underground passage to River Ouse
Open all year (ex Sat & Sun) times vary
*Tel: (0904) 59881*
National Railway Museum: displays, films, rolling stock, etc., giving comprehensive history of BR
Open all year daily 10–6 (Sun 2.30–6)
*Tel: (0904) 21261*
York Castle: two-storeyed 13th-century keep
Open all year

the 11th, a good par 5 with out of bounds to the left. A good drive threaded through the trees should keep to the fairway of the 12th, which has open fields to one side and dense rough on the right. A ditch dominates the 13th as it runs the entire length of the hole on the hooker's side. This once marked the out of bounds – it is now very much in play, with a new fence beyond.

A tight green in the corner of the club's grounds makes this a severe hole.

Players re-cross the motorway to the gorgeous 14th, played to a gorse-shrouded green with only the tip of the flag visible. There is a

stream in front of the green which might catch Fulford visitors. Pines to the right and bunkers to the left – not to speak of the prevailing wind from the right – make the 15th a difficult driving hole. Of the three holes to home, the 17th is a tester on which two massive trees come into play. The first, is to the right blocking out the hole and the other is just short of the green, which also has the stream in front to add to difficulties.

York, dominated by the facade of its imposing Minster, a cathedral which took 250 years to build, is one of the few British cities to have a campsite at its heart. Run by the Caravan

Club, this site, open to all-comers, is in four acres of parkland on the banks of the Ouse. York is a major regional centre and has been the focal point of the country's east-coast transport system for hundreds of years. Headquarters and major staging post of the London and North East Railway, running from London to Edinburgh, York is now the home of the National Railway Museum – a fascinating browse through the age of steam. John Hansom, inventor of the Hansom cab lived here too, a fact commemorated in the town's Castle Museum where you can walk the reconstructed cobbled streets of old York and gaze into shop windows of the 17th and 18th-century.

Walkers will be beckoned into the country surrounding York. To the North are the lower folds of the North Yorkshire Moors, there being particularly absorbing footpaths and signed nature trails around the White Horse of Sutton Bank near Thirsk. Anglers should head for that major Ouse tributary, the Ure, which offers trout, grayling and abundant coarse fish between Boroughbridge and Ripon. The Ouse itself, in and around York, is a fair coarse fishing river, with many opportunities for free angling (with a water authority permit).

That fading spa town of Harrogate has now become a major conference venue but it is still an attractive shopping centre beset by ornamental gardens. Nearby Knaresborough has a small zoo and an attractive setting around a gorge of the River Nidd. Famed seer and witch, Mother Shipton, who foresaw manned flight and most other 20th-century miracles, lived here and her supposed home and petrifying well can be visited.

York is the hub of a large area of weekend and holiday distractions that include three more golf courses around the city. Whether you treat it as a staging post to the delights of Scotland and the North Yorkshire coast or as a main touring base, Fulford's character may demand an extra round or two just to get the feel of the place.

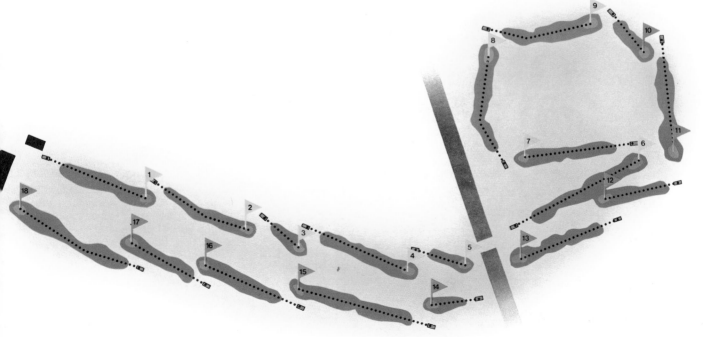

# Ganton

Ganton, Scarborough, North
Yorkshire
*Tel: Sherburn (094 44) 329*

9 miles south west of Scarborough on
A64

Gorse-covered links course: 6677yds,
SSS72

Visitors welcome weekdays only –
reservations advisable
*Professional:* P Thomson

Hotels: Crown★★★★★ Scarborough
*Tel: Scarborough (0723) 73491*
(81 rm)

Mayfair★★ Scarborough
*Tel: Scarborough (0723) 60053*
(61 rm)

Southlands★★ Scarborough
*Tel: Scarborough (0723) 61461*
(61 rm)

Walk on to the first tee at Ganton Golf Club
for the first time and you would be forgiven for
thinking that you were in fact stepping on to a
green. The reason is that all the turf on the
Ganton fairways, tees and greens is of the
finest quality. Indeed, when the hallowed turf
of Wembley stadium was badly cut by an international show-jumping event, Ganton lost its
practice ground for a few months to provide
the replacement.

Ganton is nine miles inland from the North
Yorkshire coast resort of Scarborough, a haven
of quiet by the side of the main A64 that yearly
carries hundreds of thousands of tourists to the
sandy beaches and rocky headlands of a shore
that boasts Britain's highest cliffs. At the
mouth of the Vale of Pickering, a funnel

through stunning moors, Ganton manages to
combine that wonderful turf, and the gorse and
heather of the heathland, with the gusty
breezes and sandy undersoil of a typical links.

With a history stretching back to 1891,
Ganton was soon established as a course where
history was to be made. Only five years after
the opening, the great Harry Vardon was appointed professional, a year in which he took
the first of his six Open victories. It was here,
too, that he laid the foundations for the growth
of the professional golf industry to today's
multi-million dollar status. In a £200 challenge
match against Willie Park, the first leg of
which was played at North Berwick (see pages
66 and 67), he beat the Scots master 10 and 8
to take the then-considerable pot.

Since then, Ganton has been the venue for
match after match of sterling character including the first post-war Ryder Cup match –
played to packed stands of spectators – the
PGA Matchplay Championship and the Dunlop Masters Tournament. This is not just one
of those exclusive preserves of the top-flight
golfer. Ganton opens its greens to the hundreds of touring players who come to this area
for holidays on the fascinating east coast of
Yorkshire.

A unique feature of Ganton is that, when
played from the Medal tees, it has only three
short holes at the 5th, 10th and 17th. Amateur
golfer Paul Bryan, a Member of Parliament,
managed to hole in one at two of them on one
memorable occasion. A par at any of them
would be a rewarding experience to the average
golfer – it is the 17th at which many top pros
reach for a driver when there is the suggestion
of a breath of wind about.

Ganton starts cunning and comes on fiercer.
There are bunkers and gorse in plenty to trap
the slack shot and pitching on to the reverse
slope of the 2nd green makes demands the

average golfer may be quite unprepared and
probably unable to meet.

The wind really cuts in on the 3rd, played
parallel to the practice ground and a distinct
possibility for a muscle-packed drive at 330
yards – do not attempt it when there is a breeze
in the air. Then you will be lucky to see par 4
here, as you will at the 4th on which hazard is
compounded on hazard. A gulley blocks the
fairway to the high plateau of the green, with
its large sand trap to the right. On the 5th, a
pond can be very much in play right by the
green of this 153-yard hole that Paul Bryan was
so fortunate to hit.

That pond is played over on the 6th but here
it interferes little with a good drive which will
not however be any help if it is not absolutely
as the crow flies. This is perhaps the tightest of
green entries – a pattern of traps to left and
right of the fairway that has seen many a score
card in shreds before the match is under way.

The 9th makes a formidable par 5, not so
much for its length of 496 yards but for the fact
that the Scarborough road runs parallel and
extremely close. The road is near enough to be
a bane to slicers, despite the fact that the hole
runs through a valley like a shallow ditch. It is
followed by the bunker-ringed green of the
10th, also close to the road.

Ganton's long one is the 500-yard 13th, a
long dogleg played cross-wind past a rank of
bunkers which rarely cause too much trouble.
Although the 14th seems to close in around the
green, funnelling balls into the neat impasse of
a cross bunker, it is often possible to sneak a
birdie here. This is very necessary because
Ganton's remaining par 4s will demand every
shot you can pull to keep a grip on the card.

Of them all, the 16th stands out as the most
memorable. It requires a perfect tee shot. A

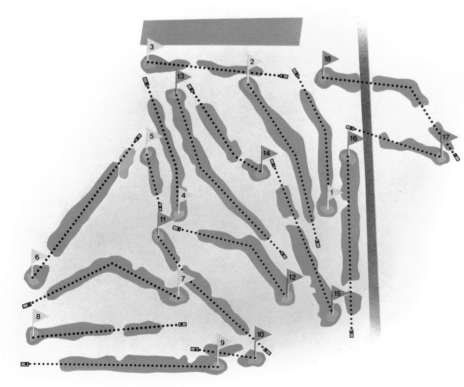

huge bunker and a tree block out the green from the left hand side of the fairway and a cluster of pine trees on the right catch anything pushed too far off the straight and narrow. The 18th is also a unique driving hole because all but the wary will drive the ball on to a road crossing the fairway. Anything to the right of this final injustice of a hole falls in the rough and fir trees block the pathway to the green from the same side. It is an end to Ganton that has seen many tournaments held in balance until the final strokes, not the least being the epic PGA Matchplay battle between Dai Rees and Max Faulkner in 1953. It was only finally resolved at the 18th.

Nearby Scarborough is a base from which to enjoy the rugged scenery of the Yorkshire coastline as well as the grandeur of the high moors behind the town. Now thought of more as a resort with razzamatazz, Scarborough once enjoyed a vogue among the chic set of Victorian and Edwardian times – the place where the bathing machine was invented to protect the modesty of increasing crowds drawn to its sun and sands. Today the twin bays around which the town straggles has all the facilities for family fun including the county's largest amusement park, which boasts a zoo, marineland and miniature railway. The park is a regular venue for the television antics of *It's a Knockout*. Scarborough itself has two fine meadow and parkland golf courses.

Out on the moors, walkers can wander free but your interest will be held by the trail notes issued for the nature trails of Ravenscar, Wykeham, Dalby and Langdale. Give your feet a rest and let the train take the strain for a day out on the Moorsrail, a steam and diesel scenic railway through a moors valley that has no road access – the terminus station is at

Pickering. There is also a locomotive shed and a gift shop close to the terminus.

Scarborough is flanked by the two great fishing ports of Whitby and Bridlington and this is some measure of the fish population on this prolific coast. Charter boats ply from Scarborough's harbour and there are good shore marks for cod, flatfish and codling around the town. There is a feast of fishing in September when the resort is the venue for nine days of competitive sea angling.

Along the coast from the quiet neighbouring resort of Filey, which still retains a genteel atmosphere, to brash Scarborough, is a string of campsites for outdoor people. Many sites have commanding views of the coast.

Ganton itself is a charming village nestling under the brow of the dale country rising to the north. A particularly attractive spot in which to reflect on a successful day's golfing is the village churchyard with its magnificent view of the Vale of Pickering.

---

**Angling**
River Derwent (upper reaches): fly fishing for trout, plus grayling Daily tickets: A Pritchard, Eastborough, Scarborough *Tel: (0723) 74017* or Everley Hotel, Hackness *Tel: (0723) 82202* Water Authority: YWA, West Riding House, 67 Albion Street, Leeds *Tel: (0532) 448201* Filey: sand fishing for most flatfish, plus good rock marks for mackerel, pollack & wrasse. Boat fishing to the south for cod & haddock Tackle shop: Dale's, 12 Hope Street, Filey *Tel: (0723) 512123*

**Camping**
Snainton: Jasmin Site ►► *Tel: (0723) 85240* Level, rural 60-pitch site (20 tents) Open Apr–Oct, must book Jul–Aug Wykeham: St Helens Caravan Park ►►►► *Tel: (0723) 862771* Partly sloping 250-pitch site (20 tents) 7m SW of Scarborough off A170 Open Mar–Oct, must book Jul–Aug

**Riding**
Snainton: Snainton Riding Centre, Snainton *Tel: (0723) 85218*

**Walking Trails**
Filey Brigg Nature Trail: 1m (1hr) coastal walk. Start from Arndale Ravine, Filey Beach (check tides)

**General**
Kirby Misperton: Flamingoland: 350-acre zoo & pleasure park, fairground, model railway – 4m S of Pickering Open Easter–Sep daily 10–4 Malton: Castle Howard: splendid 18th-century house & grounds 5m E of Malton off A64 Open Apr–Oct daily *Tel: (065 384) 333* Roman Museum: extensive collections from Roman settlements in region Open all year (ex Sun mornings) *Tel: (0653) 4941 ext 67* Pickering: North Yorkshire Moors Railway ('Moorsrail'): 18m track, loco shed, gift shop Open easter–early Nov *Tel: (0751) 72508/ 73535* Pickering castle: 12th-century stronghold Open all year Scarborough: Scarborough Zoo & Marineland: many attractions including bears, dolphins, monkeys & sealions Open Easter–Oct 10–dusk *Tel: (0723) 64401*

---

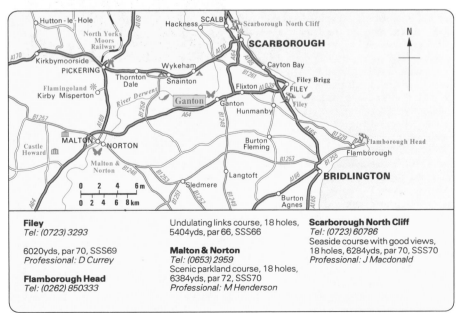

**Filey**
*Tel: (0723) 3293*

6020yds, par 70, SSS69
*Professional: D Currey*

**Flamborough Head**
*Tel: (0262) 850333*

Undulating links course, 18 holes, 5404yds, par 66, SSS66

**Malton & Norton**
*Tel: (0653) 2959*
Scenic parkland course, 18 holes, 6384yds, par 72, SSS70
*Professional: M Henderson*

**Scarborough North Cliff**
*Tel: (0723) 60786*
Seaside course with good views, 18 holes, 6284yds, par 70, SSS70
*Professional: J Macdonald*

# Bamburgh Castle

Bamburgh Castle,
Bamburgh, Northumberland
*Tel: Bamburgh (066 84) 378*

From Belford on A1, 3 miles east on
B1342

Beautiful seaside course: 5495yds,
SSS67

Visitors welcome by prior telephone
appointment

Hotels: Dunes★★ Seahouses
*Tel: Seahouses (0665) 720378*
(30 rm)

Lord Crewe Arms★★ Bamburgh
*Tel: Bamburgh (066 84) 243*
(26 rm)

Sunningdale★
*Tel: Bamburgh (066 84) 334*
(18 rm)

That the north east of England has more than one golf course laid out under the gaze of a castle is probably no coincidence. Fortresses naturally have to stand on high ground and it is military commonsense to make some clearance of the field of fire on the lower ground outside the walls. What this operation leaves behind is an undulating meadow dotted with the more senior trees and as fitted for excellent golf as any parkland anywhere. That the aristocratic owners of such fortresses were often the very people whose leisure thoughts turned to golf is another commonplace in the history of the Royal and Ancient game.

Bamburgh Castle, a craggy citadel of the Northumberland coast, close to the border actions that characterised this area's pre-occupation with the Scots and a commanding presence to invaders choosing a sea route, dates back to AD547. It was a Royal lodge and archaeological evidence shows the site has been occupied since the 1st-century BC. This awe-inspiring stronghold is the focal point of most vantage spots on the Bamburgh Castle golf course, which has a very recent provenance indeed compared with its neighbour. The course was laid out in 1904, a three-quarter century of golf that was celebrated in 1979 by the extensive modernisation of the clubhouse. Golfers who have played the world over and have, perhaps by accident, hit on Bamburgh, have to admit that for sheer breathtaking beauty this gem of a course has few equals. When one stands on the 15th tee, the panorama includes the Castle itself and its golden sands to the right, the Farne Islands occupy the centre stage and Budle Bay curves round to the left. It is also a golf course that is great fun to play. At 5465 yards, Bamburgh is the shortest course featured in this guide but there are no apologies to make – it is quite simply holiday golf at its best.

Short the course may be, but with a par of 68, few visitors will conquer it in the first round or two. There are six par 3 holes and all

are, to the say the least, intriguing. Take the first, well-named 'The Dinkie' because the winter of 1978 saw snow and ice nibble a couple of yards from the dunes which eat into the land between the course and the sea. There is a strong sense of isolation on the tee with a virtual void to the front and the rocks and sand beckoning to the right – strong medicine on a 182-yard hole. Another par 3 follows called 'Picnic Bay' for one looks down on the right over many families taking lunch. The wind – and on this stretch of the coast it can be a howler on the sunniest of days – may make its 213 yards difficult to cover with a driver. Then you are hurled into a formidable par 5 of 510 yards, aptly called 'The Quarry' for the huge rocky face to the left upon which a raucous chorus of gulls signal their displeasure at any

kind of disturbance. A wall is a long carry ahead and the green is uphill. Gaining the 4th, a par 5 of only 476 yards may feel like relief to some but the green is hidden and the view becomes distracting. To the front is Mount Cheviot which lends its name to the hole, and to the right one looks over Budle Bay, a great inlet in the coast which is home to countless species of birds and other wildlife.

Ferns surround the 5th tee, a delightful setting but one which is eclipsed on the 6th. This is a par 3 of 224 yards but it must be almost unique in having a stroke play of one over its uphill fairway to a plateau green. It is driveable only by single figure players and a lottery to the majority of visitors. While the 7th actually lays claim to the name 'Rockies', it is a more justified description of the 8th, with its bowl

*Bamburgh Castle*

landscape by Russell Flint depicting the 12th tee's view of Lindisfarne, which should not distract you from the testing 413-yard length. An uphill fairway makes the 13th, at 406 yards, play a lot longer. Accuracy counts here as rocks bound the left, gorse is to the right and drystone walls around the green.

The short 14th replays the 8th in the opposite direction, uphill, and so to the fabulous 15th from where the massive Castle rears up to dominate the tiny village and a ravine guards the 404-yard hole for a tricky par 4. Off the back tee of the 16th, a guide pole signals the optimum line to avoid an impossible lie in the hillside heather. Following up is a 17th of just 260 yards, which is, however, a frightener. One drives between a fern-covered hill on the left, which is the back of the quarry, and a drystone wall marking a field out of bounds on the left – a narrow passage with little room for error. Judging by the number of poachers who have been sighted on the 18th, the rabbits are prolific – although the hole is called 'Harelaw'. Played at castle level, the green is appropriately well-guarded, but for its 314-yard length a long iron will suit most players.

Despite the high population of rabbits, sea angling remains number two sport (and to non-anglers, one of the most exacting places to fish anywhere). Codling is the main target which can be caught throughout the year, but the keynote to a successful day's sport is studying the rock marks at low water.

Given warm weather, the Northumberland coast offers the best sunbathing in the country, with miles of unspoilt and deserted beaches. While above, the springy turf and bracing air encourage long clifftop walks overlooking the restless waters of the North Sea. A respect of the sea is further engendered at the Grace Darling Museum at Bamburgh, where visitors are reminded of a successful attempt by Grace and her father (who was Keeper of the Longstone lighthouse) to save the lives of five people.

Less eventful boat trips are available to the Farne Islands, once the home of St Aidan and St Cuthbert, and now the breeding ground for seabirds, or from the 12th-century castle at

green set about by rocky spurs and high banks. It is a first leg that is completed by the awesome 9th built over a rock outcrop with more gorgeous views. Its 361 yards bespeak a modest par 4 but do not be deceived – there is a jagged ravine guarding the green.

A little romantically, one feels, the short, 196-yard 10th has the name 'Fox Coverts' – the green is partially blind and players ring a bell when it is clear. The 'Fox Coverts' actually present more of a hazard on the succeeding hole on which a drive of at least 150 yards down the middle is required to dodge the foxes or the heather and gorse to the left. Your problems will not yet be ended, as the hole is a dogleg and the green lies between a hill and a five-barred gate alongside the Budle Bay road.

In Bamburgh's clubhouse is a remarkable

### Angling
**Alnwick:** Tackle shop: Alnwick Sports Centre, Narrowgate
*Tel: (0665) 604462*
**Seahouses:** pier & harbour spots for codling, flatfish & whiting. Boat fishing near Farne Is. may yield cod, dogfish & gurnard
**River Tweed** (lower reaches): fine salmon & sea trout plus good roach
Free fishing from Horncliffe to estuary

### Camping
**Bamburgh:** Beadnell Links ▶▶▶
*Tel: (066 589) 241*
10-pitch (no tents) farmland site
Open Apr–Oct, must book Jul–Aug
**Glororum Caravan Park** ▶▶
*Tel: (066 84) 205*
Pleasant 100-pitch site (no tents)
Open Apr–Oct, must book Jul–Aug
**Belford:** Waren Caravan Site ▶▶▶
*Tel: (066 84) 366*
105-pitch site (no tents) 4m W of Bamburgh
Open May–Oct, no bookings
**Wooler:** Bridge End Caravan Site ▶▶▶
*Tel: (066 82) 447*
Grassy 55-pitch site (25 caravans)
Open Mar–Oct, must book Jul–Aug

### General
**Bamburgh:** Bamburgh Castle: imposing Norman fortress

Open Apr–Sep afternoons only, for party tours
*Tel: (066 84) 208*
Grace Darling Museum: documents & relics of the 19th-century heroine
Open Apr–Sep daily 11–7
**Berwick-upon-Tweed:** Museum & Art Gallery: local antiquities, brasswork & ceramics plus French school paintings
Open Jun–Sep Mon–Fri 2–5 (Sat 10–1)
*Tel: (0289) 7320*
**Chillingham:** Chillingham Wild Cattle: park containing herd of notable wild white cattle, 10m SW of Bamburgh off B6348
Open Apr–Oct (ex Tue & Sun morning)
*Tel: (066 85) 213/250*
**Embleton:** Dunstanburgh Castle: remains of 14th-century fortress, on coast 9m S of Bamburgh. Accessible all year
**Ford:** Heatherslaw Mill: one of the earliest water-driven flour mills still operable, 7m E of Coldstream off B6353
Open Apr–Oct daily 11–6
*Tel: (089 082) 338*
**Lindisfarne** (or Holy Is): Lindisfarne Priory: very early Christian church only accessible at low tide
*Tel: (0289) 87200*

Warkworth to a hermitage chapel skilfully cut out of solid rock.

The outdoor life can be more fully enjoyed by choosing a camping holiday at one of several well-run sites close to the wild coastal beauty of this area.

*Note: No official course map is available.*

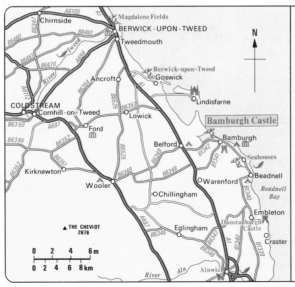

### Alnwick
Parkland course with plenty of trees, 9 holes, 5403yds, par 66, SSS66

### Berwick-upon-Tweed (Goswick)
*Tel: (0289) 87256*
Easily walked links course, 18 holes, 6437yds, par 72, SSS71

### Magdalene Fields (Berwick-upon-Tweed)
Exposed seaside course with natural hazards, 18 holes, 6551yds, par 72, SSS71

### Seahouses
*Tel: (0665) 720794*
Pleasant seaside course 4m SE of Bamburgh off B1340, 18 holes, 5400yds, par 67, SSS67

# Royal Lytham & St Annes and St Annes Old Links

Royal Lytham and St Annes, Links Gate, St Annes on Sea, Lancashire
*Tel: St Annes (0253) 724206*

St Annes Old Links, Highbury Road, St Annes on Sea
*Tel: St Annes (0253) 723597*

Royal Lytham and St Annes

1 mile from centre of St Annes on Sea

Attractive tree-studded links course: 6822yds, SSS73

Visitors welcome by advance letter or telephone or with membership, restricted to Mondays, Tuesdays, Wednesdays, Thursdays and Fridays
*Professional:* E Musty

St Annes Old Links

Windy seaside links: 6601yds, SSS72

Visitors welcome by advance letter or telephone but restricted
*Professional:* D Stewart

Hotels: Chadwick★★ St Annes
*Tel: St Annes (0253) 720061*
(50 rm)

Clifton Arms★★★★ Lytham
*Tel: St Annes (0253) 739898*

Fernlea★★ St Annes
*Tel: St Annes (0253) 726726*
(92 rm)

Royal Lytham & St Annes has a unique place in the history of British golf – it is the only championship course on which European and Commonwealth players have held off the challenge of the American professionals in the Open. Since 1926 when the legendary US amateur, Bobby Jones, took the first Lytham Open, players from the States have had a thin time. On this great course, an emerald of turf set in the midst of an expansive residential suburb and flanked by the main Blackpool railway and Lytham's red-brick station, great battles have been fought.

In 1963's Open, New Zealander Bob Charles became the first left-handed golfer to take a major title and in 1969 Royal Lytham was the scene of Tony Jacklin's emotional and very welcome win after a gap of eighteen years had elapsed since the last British winner. Only recently it was the flamboyant brilliance of Severiano Ballesteros that thrilled an enorm-

ous crowd drawn to the 1979 Open. Despite missing many fairways and playing from an area reserved for parked cars – among several other mishaps – Ballesteros' play never failed to grip the gallery.

It was forty years before Royal Lytham attained the status it enjoys today. The club was founded in 1886, a year after the first-ever Amateur Championship had been played at Royal Liverpool. Contemporary pictures show that the sand dunes stretched inland for more than half a mile of windswept hinterland. It was on the furthermost edge of this desert that the first course was laid down, long before the spread of houses made its way down to this part of the Ribble's estuary. Nothing man-made can destroy the charm of this oasis of golf, which is undeniably a links in character, with its well-drained sand and trees which share that weathered bent of storm-battered and salt-shrivelled trees everywhere. At 6697 yards Lytham is among the shortest of the major championship courses but there are plenty of interesting hazards among its barely disguised sand dunes. To many visitors off the forward tees who are enjoying a trip on top form, some of the holes may appear less demanding than they ought to. Just try it from the back, tiger tees for a flavour of what the professionals are up against – Royal Lytham & St Annes is not a course on which anyone can scramble a good score.

Like many courses, there is a gentle lead into the play on the 1st – a mere 200 yards or so for a par 3 that will not stretch too many players. The 2nd and 3rd present the challenge of the railway immediately to the right of their long-legged par 4 lengths. This threat of the out of

bounds always tends to make the visitor play away from trouble – into a number of well-placed traps, of course.

The railway intrudes again on the 7th, one of Lytham's great par 5s, with a healthy 553-yard length and a very necessary dogleg around some deep traps. Very few players will reach the green in two around these cleverly placed bunkers waiting to catch the slice. The railway plays its part again on the 8th, which also suffers from a lane all-too-eager to take your tee-shot if it has fallen short and a guard bunker barring anything other than a spot-on pitch to the plateau green. A short par 3 brings

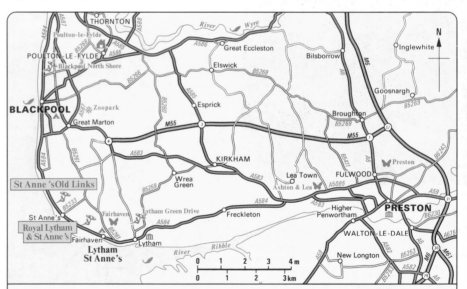

**Ashton & Lea**
*Tel: (0772) 726480*
Testing heathland course 5m W of Preston, 18 holes, 6286yds, par 71, SSS70
*Professional: J Gove*

**Blackpool North Shore**
*Tel: (0253) 52054*
Rolling parkland course, 18 holes, 6433yds, par 72, SSS71
*Professional: C Rigby*

**Fairhaven**
*Tel: (0253) 736741*
Flattish parkland course 1m W of Lytham village, 18 holes, 6885yds, par 74, SSS73
*Professional: W Miller*

**Lytham Green Drive**
*Tel: (0253) 737390*
Seaside course well-suited to tourists, 18 holes, 582 yds, par 69, SSS68
*Professional: H Beck*

**Poulton-le-Fylde**
*Tel: (0253) 886831*
Easily walked municipal course, 9 holes, 2751yds, par 33, SSS66
*Professional: B Ward*

**Preston**
*Tel: (0772) 700011*
Interesting countryside course 3m N of Preston, 18 holes, 6300yds, par 72, SSS70
*Professional: M Greenwood*

*Royal Lytham & St Annes*

you into the narrow corner of the club's grounds before making back towards the clubhouse itself.

Starting for this haven of battered players is a short par 4 on which the drive is critical because of the sand-dunes on each side of the fairway. The newly-designed tee gives the hole that much more distance. The 11th is a good par 5 which doglegs to the left, followed by a nasty par 3 of 200 yards. Anything not carried to the middle of the green will be snapped up by a bunker and too generous a stroke finished in the road, out of bounds.

This is the prelude to Royal Lytham's stunning finale. The 13th is a tremendous par 4 demanding pin-point accuracy from the tee. A long iron or wood second shot must be steered clear of fairway lining bunkers and traps to the left of the green. The 15th is another superb par 4, which doglegs to the right and requires two healthy shots to get on to the putting surface. On the right is heather and on the left some heavy rough. A short par 4 16th gives some respite before hitting the 17th, a great hole. Thick rough and sand bounds it to the left and two bunkers make a very difficult narrow green entry.

A spectacular finish is provided by the 18th.

The green lies in the clubhouse shadow from which the verandah gives thronging spectators a fine view of the drama. Those who saw Jacklin drive this hole for victory gasped when the ball soared and landed true in the middle of the fairway, safely away from the bunker traps.

A visit to this part of the country would not be complete without at least a sight of St Annes Old Links, the club that since 1901 has vied with Royal Lytham as a major attraction of this coast. Laid out on essentially similar terrain to its rival, the Old Links never was such a stiff test of golf but with its fine greens and rolling fairways it has been a popular venue for Open championship qualifying rounds. This wind-blown course, also renowned for its excellent clubhouse facilities, features three very long holes, the 5th, 17th and 18th, and is at its most demanding on the short par 3 9th.

Lytham St Annes is the engagingly more sedate satellite resort of that Mecca of the north west coast, Blackpool. It is laid out like a garden city and has a considerable number of less highly powered attractions such as the yacht harbour in the old port area of the dock creek, the windmill on Lytham Green and the Motive Power Museum and Lytham Creek Railway. Here are preserved trams and engines with weekend rides on a short length of track. Lytham's beach is firm sand, bordered by attractive dunes.

Blackpool is one of Britain's largest resorts and one that sets out to offer all the fun of the fair for its millions of visitors. The town has seven miles of promenade bordering safe beaches and has three piers – and, of course, the Tower soaring over the internationally famous Tower Ballroom. It has a season of non-stop entertainment and numbers among its chief attractions the enormous Pleasure Beach Amusement Park, the illuminations (September and October) and the Golden Mile of amusement arcades.

Surprisingly it is possible to escape into the tranquillity of the countryside. Beacon Fell Country Park, eight miles north of nearby Preston, features panoramic views over to the Forest of Bowland and the distant smudge of the Lake District, forest walks and a short nature trail. On the coast between Blackpool and Morecambe there is some very fine sea angling to be had – beach casting can yield cod,

**Angling**
Blackpool: beach fishing for cod, dab, flounder & pouting, but tends to be overcrowded. Better sites are St Annes & Fairhaven on Ribble estuary
Tackle shop: Nicholson's, Warley Road, Blackpool
*Tel: (0253) 22557*
River Wyre: good game fishing plus quality chub & roach
Daily tickets: Ribble & Wyre Fisheries Association (G Jones), 1 Carnarvon Road, Preston
Water Authority: NWWA, New Town House, Buttermarket Street, Warrington
*Tel: (0925) 53999*

**Camping**
Blackpool: Cropper Caravan Park ►►
*Tel: (0253) 62051*
Flat 121-pitch site (no tents)
Open Mar–Oct, must book
Marton Mere Leisure Centre ►►►
*Tel: (0253) 64280*
Large 650-pitch site (no tents)
Open Mar–Oct, no bookings
Lytham St Annes: Eastham Hall Caravan Site ►►►►
*Tel: (0253) 737907*
Rural 250-pitch site (no tents)
Open Mar–Oct, must book Jul–Aug

**General**
Blackpool: Dr Who Exhibition: Tardis plus many of the TV hero's enemies
Open May–Oct daily from 10 (weekends only in winter)
*Tel: (0253) 22005*
Grundy Art Gallery: permanent display of 19th/20th-century painters
Open all year 10–5 (ex Sun)
*Tel: (0253) 23977*
Tower Buildings & Circus: large complex including ballroom, children's farm & aquarium
Open May–Oct daily 9.30–11pm
*Tel: (0253) 25252*
Zoopark: collection of small mammals & birds plus miniature railway & picnic area
Open all year
*Tel: (0253) 65027*
Fleetwood: Thornton Pottery: stoneware, earthenware & ceramic jewellery
Open Jun–Dec daily 2–5
*Tel: (0253) 855045*
Lytham: Lytham Motive Power Museum: vintage cars, locomotives & aircraft
Open mid-May–mid-Oct daily 11–5 (ex Mon & Fri)
*Tel: (0253) 733122*
St Annes: St Annes Art Gallery: regular exhibitions by local artists
Open all year (ex Sat & Sun)

flounder, plaice and whiting. Fleetwood is the best centre for boat fishing. Campers will find five sites from Lytham to Fleetwood, two of them offering a full range of facilities.

Lytham St Annes other claim to fame, other than golf, is that it has for many years been the base of Ernie the Premium Bond computer. When your number comes up it would be fitting to spend a little of that bounty on the distinctive golf that Lytham's dunes provide.

**ROYAL LYTHAM & ST ANNES GOLF COURSE**

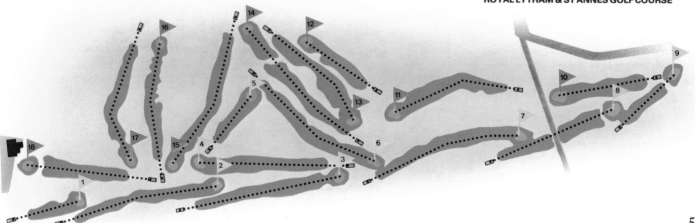

# Royal Liverpool

Royal Liverpool, Meols Drive,
Hoylake, Wirral, Merseyside
*Tel: Liverpool 051 – 632 3101*

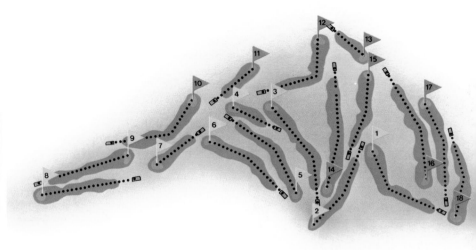

10 miles west of Liverpool on A553

Windswept, seaside links course:
6737yds, SSS74

Visitors welcome with letter of
introduction
*Professional:* J Morgan

Hotels: Bowler Hat★★★Oxton,
Birkenhead
*Tel: Liverpool 051 – 652 4931*
(29 rm)

Central★★★ Clifton Crescent,
Birkenhead
*Tel: Liverpool 051 – 647 6347*
(34 rm)

Dee★★ West Kirby
*Tel: Liverpool 051 – 625 5532*
(10 rm)

Stanley★★ Hoylake
*Tel: Liverpool 051 – 625 5532*
(10 rm)

Royal Liverpool, a club almost universally known by the course location, Hoylake, is situated on that extraordinary limb of industrialised flatland, Cheshire's Wirral, some ten miles south of the mouth of the Mersey. It is the course that saw the start of the Amateur Championship in 1885 and was a regular venue for the Open Championship until 1967. This was the year in which the Open was taken by Roberto Vicenzo, who won for himself a special admiration for his skills and Argentinian charm. Previous Open winners at Hoylake include some of the legendary names of golf – J H Taylor took one of his five wins there, Bobby Jones, well on the way to his grand slam was another Hoylake champion, as were Walter Hagan and Australia's Peter Thomson.

Hoylake has other footholds in the history of the game. It was on its wind-blown links, which have little or no shelter from the prevailing wind batting in across the Irish Sea, that John Ball and Harold Hilton, two of Britain's most talented amateurs learned their golf. In 1902, using one of the new Haskell balls, Alexander Herd took the Open title and sealed the fate of the guttie ball. Five years later Arnaud Massey of France battled through a dreadful gale to record the Open's first foreign victory.

Although it is now thirteen years since the Open came to the Wirral, the famous links continues to host major amateur championships and international representatives' matches. John Morgan, who is the club's current professional, has represented Britain and Ireland on several occasions in the 'mini' Ryder Cup tournament.

The qualities of Hoylake, because of its relatively flat terrain and sparse vegetation are not easily appreciated by new players to the course.

The prevailing wind causes problems for even the best players, who would readily admit it is a course which must be played many times before its true value as a testing course can really be appreciated.

It is said that Hoylake has two of the best holes in British golf, at the 1st and the 7th. The opener is, in fact, one of the most difficult starts to a match in the game. It is a par 4 of 424 yards with a dogleg right and out of bounds all the way up to and beyond the green on the right – thick rough bounds the left. Many cards can be ruined at the very outset of the round by a couple of shots that are less than perfect – a full 240-yard drive at least is required to reach the dogleg alone.

With that ordeal over, the second hole may be viewed as fair game for a par 4. The 3rd, too, is a relatively straightforward par 5, although it is heavily bunkered around the green – and it was this hole more than any other that paved the way to Vicenzo's Open victory. He made two eagle threes and two birdie fours there in the championship. A gentle par 3 is followed by a short par 4 and then things start to become

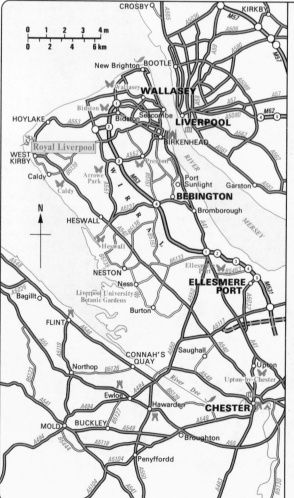

**Arrowe Park (Birkenhead)**
*Tel: (051 677) 1527*
Pleasant parkland course, 18
holes, 5853yds, par 68, SSS68
*Professional: S Wilson*

**Bidston**
*Tel: (051 638) 3412*
Breezy parkland course 2m SW of
Wallasey off A551, 18 holes,
6207yds, par 71, SSS70
*Professional: P Bramall*

**Caldy**
*Tel: (051 625) 5660*
Long parkland course 2m SE of
West Kirby, 18 holes, 6642yds,
par 71, SSS72
*Professional: G Roberts*

**Ellesmere Port**
*Tel: (051 339) 7689*
Park course with many hazards,
18 holes, 6599yds, par 72, SSS71
*Professional: W Sutherland*

**Heswall**
*Tel: (051 342) 1237*
Undulating parkland course 5m S
of Birkenhead, 18 holes,
6216yds, par 71, SSS70
*Professional: A Thompson*

**Prenton (Birkenhead)**
*Tel: (051 608) 1053*
Easily walked parkland course, 18
holes, 6324yds, par 71, SSS70
*Professional: R Jarman*

**Upton-by-Chester**
*Tel: (0244) 23638*
Pleasant, but testing parkland
course 2m N of Chester, 18
holes, 5847yds, par 69, SSS68
*Professional: P Gardner*

**Wallasey**
*Tel: (051 639) 3700*
Old links course, 18 holes,
6607yds, par 72, SSS73
*Professional: W Hallam*

*Speke Hall near Liverpool*

more difficult on the 6th, where the drive must be hit over a guide post and anything hooked into the left is out of bounds.

One of the most treacherous holes in British golf, the short 7th is 201 yards from the championship tee, with an out of bounds all the way down the left. Anything actually pitched to the left hand side of the green will automatically finish out of bounds, too. One Cheshire player, in a play-off for the County championship took eleven here after hitting the green every time.

With that severe test over, the player can afford to relax a little, although both the 8th and 9th can play two wood shots to the green if the wind is howling – a shortfall on the 8th, in particular, leaves you with a very difficult pitch to the green.

Homeward-bound, the next four holes offer superb views over the sea and, to the landward side, a panorama of the club and clubhouse. The 13th tee, with the sea beyond, can play anything from a wedge to a four iron depending on the wind. The deep bunkers present a major problem on this short hole – anything placed too far to the left tends to land in a garden from where, it is said, some 2000 balls were retrieved over a period of four years.

The wind holds sway on the 15th, too, making it one of the most difficult holes at Hoylake – the green may be unreachable with two drivers. Nevertheless it *is* a par 5. En route, players have to negotiate cavernous bunkers from the tee and then bunkers again, standing guard on the green, while a trip off the fairway lands you in thick rough.

It is the penultimate hole that is the sting in Hoylake's tail. It is a critical driving hole, with out of bounds on the right and a dogleg to shave on the left. The green lies very close to the boundary wire of Stanley Road and to a line-up of bunkers sealing off any approach from the left.

Once the fairway bunkers have been missed by the drive on the last hole, the player is left with a medium iron to gain the generous green, which is as good an example of Hoylake's velvety putting turf as any on this beautifully-prepared course. The average visitor will then be well aware of Hoylake's championship quality and be thankful for the safety of a clubhouse which is rich in the traditions and atmosphere of the game.

Hoylake itself (which also boasts another 18-hole course designed by James Braid) is a largely residential resort and was once a port for Ireland. A beach and two-mile promenade may provide amusements enough for a holidaying family when combined with picnics at the Red Rocks and swimming in the town's pool. Nearby, West Kirby gives views across the Dee estuary to the distant mountains of North Wales – from here it is possible to walk (at low tide) to the bird-thronged offshore islets of the estuary. There are even seals on Hilbre.

Major resort of the Wirral peninsula is New Brighton, connected to Liverpool, across the mouth of the Mersey, by a regular ferry service. Other boat trips from Seacombe Ferry include the cruises of the *Royal Iris*, a pleasure boat with bars and discos which plies the Mersey ports. All the attractions of a major resort are here, including a particularly traffic-free promenade, an enormous outdoor swimming pool with its own artificial beach and a packed season's calendar of events such as power boat racing, sailing regattas and other sporting events. Beaches here are sandy but there is a lot

of tidal movement and it is often quite a walk to the water's edge. Behind New Brighton is the extensive Wirral Country Park – undulating land with views over the Dee.

Cod, dab, flounder and whiting can be taken from the many excellent shore fishing marks around the Wirral, which include Thurstaston, the Caldey Channel, off the Marine Lake at West Kirby, and along the New Brighton promenade. Worm baits are available locally at several tackle shops.

The Wirral, and its great golf course of Hoylake, is well served by good roads such as the M53 motorway, which brings the more attractive resort tip within easy driving distance of Cheshire and the holiday centres of the North Wales coast. Even if you feel the Wirral's limited attractions are not worth a stay in the area, a day's tour will suffice to enjoy Hoylake's many diversions.

# Royal Birkdale, Formby and Hillside

Royal Birkdale, Waterloo House, Southport, Merseyside
*Tel: Southport (0704) 69903*

Formby, Golf Road, Formby, Liverpool, Merseyside
*Tel: Formby (070 48) 72164*

Hillside, Hastings Road, Southport, Merseyside
*Tel: Southport (0704) 67169*

---

Royal Birkdale

2 miles south of Stockport

Championship course: 6711yds, SSS74
*Course designer:* George Low, later modified by Fred G Hawtree and J H Taylor

Visitors welcome, reservation advisable
*Professional:* R Halsall

Formby

1 mile west of A565 by Freshfield Station

Championship links course: 6700yds, SSS73

Visitors welcome, reservation advisable, restricted Wednesdays and weekends
*Professional:* C Harrison

Hillside

South of Southport ½ mile from Hillside Station

Windy links course: 6850yds, SSS73

Visitors welcome but restricted Tuesday mornings, weekends and Bank Holidays
*Professional:* J Hewitt

Hotels: Bold★★ Southport
*Tel: Southport (0704) 32578*
(29 rm)

Prince of Wales★★★★ Southport
*Tel: Southport (0704) 36688*
(117 rm)

Royal Clifton★★★ Southport
*Tel: Southport (0704) 33771*
(117 rm)

---

Matching the courses of the Wirral dunelands to the south of the Mersey are a string of links pearls to the north of the mighty river's mouth. Formby, Hillside and that prince among championship courses, Royal Birkdale, are all strung within five miles of each other on the hills and sands of the Southport coast. A visit to this location would hardly be complete with-

out a sample of all three and here they are contrasted.

The amazingly quick rise of Royal Birkdale to its position of eminence as one of the most popular and demanding championship courses in Britain is a triumph of both design and groundsmanship. Founded at the turn of the century, the original design was by George Low who, rather cleverly at the time, ignored the temptation of utilising the many slopes of the giant sandhills here and laid out his fairways in the flat valleys. There have been many alterations made to Birkdale since, notably by F G Hawtree and J H Taylor, but the principle remains the same and it has allowed successive changes to keep abreast of modern golfers' techniques and abilities. Not the least consideration is that the hilltops can be occupied by spectators and Birkdale may well be Britain's best course for viewing golfing thrills.

It was not until 1935 that the course, already with a reputation for great golf on a coastline rich with such opportunities, first hosted a major championship. It was a modest start – the English Ladies Championship – and since then Birkdale has been the venue for most events in the calendar.

Just over 7000 yards from the championship tees, Birkdale is a magnificent test of golf. It is not just one of the longest courses in British golf, it is also one of the toughest. Among its many trials, the finishing four holes are as demanding as any in the world. Veteran Royal Birkdale professional Bob Halsall, who retired in 1979 after a lifetime of service for the club, always maintained that anyone taking level fours on them in the final round of an Open was the winner. He was rarely proved wrong.

Royal Birkdale has it all. Each hole is

beautifully balanced and demands the player's complete repertoire of skills. It probably has the most difficult set of par 3s in top-class tournament play because the prevailing winds rarely go full with or against the shot – it is a fierce crosswind all the way.

The 1st used to be a gentle canter of a par 5 but as a 450-yard par 4 it is a really tough starter. The 2nd is genuinely easier if you can avoid the guard bunkers at the green, while the 3rd is blind to the extent that you cannot see the base of the flag and fairway bunkers creep in from the right. There are just 202 yards of the 4th and it is one of Birkdale's great tests. Generous bunkering of the green and extremely deceptive windage make it a hard-won par 3. Most top players err on the safe side at the 5th, using a one iron from the tee but it will play for a birdie in good conditions.

Players have two distinct options on the 6th, a spectacular hole. You can lay up short of the mid-fairway cross bunkers or go for the big drive to set up an easier second on this right-hand dogleg.

Take the safe course and you will have to thread the second shot through a testing nest of bunkers.

Club selection is vital for the 7th, a short hole of about 150 yards that is a minefield of bunkers (one of them, unusually, has an island in it to prevent erosion). From the semi-sheltered tee, the ball flies some 40 feet above the green to be buffeted by the wind. The 8th is noted for its tricky putting slope. The only wholly blind drive on the course is at the 9th, a par 4 of 400 yards or so with a dogleg right to a green with a very well-guarded entrance.

Starting for home, players have to avoid mounds to the left and a large bunker to the

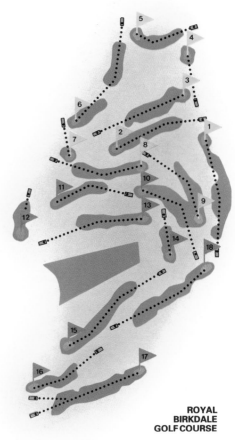

**ROYAL
BIRKDALE
GOLF COURSE**

right to gain little more than a pitch to the 10th green which is a saddle.

From holes 13 to 15 you skirt Birkdale's enormous practice ground to the finale. Most professionals would hope to take the 13th green in two shots for a straightforward par 5 and on to the wicked short 14th. The green itself is heavily trapped, with bunkers to the left being particularly dangerous. The tee shot is terribly exposed and the green falls from the left hand front edge to the back.

Counted among the top eighteen holes of golf, the 15th has a demanding tee shot which must steer clear of three left hand bunkers in line. More fairway traps greet the second shot of this 540-yard par 5 and the green is in a nest of bunkers. A carry of some 230 yards from the tee is demanded on the 16th before you can clear the dogleg and shoot over further cross bunkers. The drive on the 17th has to find the fairway through two huge sentinel dunes with fairway bunkers to follow. Bunkers to the right dominate the last hole which is a slight dogleg to the right, running a gauntlet of traps for a par 5. The hole usually plays downwind but tension is held to the end by a ridged green.

Birkdale has, of course, been the scene of many memorable tussles. Lee Trevino just sneaked a victory here over 'Mr Lu' in 1971, when he was five strokes clear of the field – and then took a 7 on the treacherous 17th to win by only one stroke. This was the hole on which Jacklin took only three strokes in 1969's Ryder Cup to pull up to Nicklaus – the game was halved when Nicklaus conceded a putt that anyone could have missed. Arnold Palmer drove a ball (and a chunk of the bush it lay under) some 140 yards to carry his second shot to the green and eventually ward off the threat

of Dai Rees – a plaque on the 16th green marks this event of the 1961 Open.

Only five miles to the south is the course of Formby, completely different in character from Birkdale. This club, which has a ladies course designed inside the main links, is on grounds of staggering beauty, with scenic woodlands, pine trees and superb fairways. The sea is only visible from the courses mid-point so you would be forgiven for thinking that Formby could be a piece of parkland. That it is not, for those considerable hillocks are all sand to the core and the grass of the greens and fairways is very links-like in character, so is the wind.

Formby, originally founded in 1884, has a course, lying in the valleys of the hills, that was first laid out by W Park and then modified by Harry Colt. It has a considerable length of 6700 yards, with just three par 5s and three par 3s. Many of the holes have an innocuous character at first glance but do not be taken in.

The 3rd, of over 500 yards for par 5, is the first of Formby's spectacular holes you meet. The fairway tumbles to a green set before a backdrop of pines. The drive must be cute enough to dodge the left-hand bunkers or placed smartly and safely to the right before a second shot that has to avoid a pair of cross bunkers. Of the short holes, the 9th is the one to watch. From a high tee, the sea can be viewed over the green and the wind will undoubtedly be in your face. It is some 182 yards, perhaps a safe carry with a wood or long iron, but then sand surrounds the green and accuracy is essential to thread this needle. On the return, the 12th is notable as one of those holes playing interminably longer than its 407 yards along an undulating fairway to a smooth green.

Formby's final green is some 80 yards long,

reached over a switchback fairway with heavy bunkering to each side.

The third of this coast's great triumvirate is Hillside sitting neatly between Formby and Birkdale. New to the arena of first class events, it was not until 1965 that Hillside staged its first international. It was the event in which Walter Danecki set the golf world giggling by bluffing his way into an Open qualifier as a professional and topped the 100 on two successive rounds. He later admitted to being a Milwaukee telephone engineer on holiday. An extensive redesign of most of the courses's second half, which is similar in its sandhill terrain to Birkdale, has made Hillside a venue to be reckoned with.

Hillside's principal test is the four par 5s, all topping 500 yards and the 17th being nearly 550 yards. Few players venture to put the ball on the green in two. That is not to say the short holes are not a supreme test too. The 147-yard 10th is the classic, with its green raised above the tee backed by a massive sandhill and edged by trees. Depending on the wind, this can take a long iron or a fair crack with a wood. Wind is also the decider at the short 4th. Here the tee is sheltered by a tree windbreak which often confuses iron selection. As soon as the ball is caught by the breeze, it tends to pull the ball down. The result of these contrasts is a course that has the rare ability of keeping the good drivers on a par with the short-hole marksmen.

Like Formby, Hillside is bounded by the Liverpool Southport railway, a hazard to the habitual hooker on the first two holes. The 3rd

**FORMBY
GOLF COURSE**

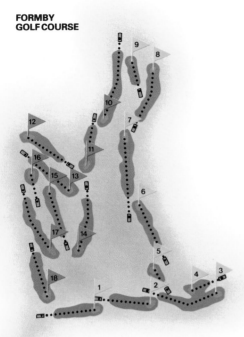

doglegs back to a nest of bunkers around the green before you meet the wicked 4th. On the homeward run, the 11th is a hole of hard truth, however buoyant you may feel about the score on the 10th. It has a wide fairway at first sight but its 508 yards demand all of three good drives from the average player and there is a distinct funnelling effect between the sandhills which line the green.

Hillside's final three holes incorporate all that is good about the course. A par 3 16th of nearly 200 yards demands a powerful and accurate drive, the 17th is that tiger of a hole and the 18th wings downhill on a dogleg around some very retentive rough. It is a fine end to a superb course.

Six miles of golden sands and dunes,

ornamental gardens and a very large lake for watersports has helped to make Southport a lively and popular resort. The pier, at three-quarters of a mile the longest in Britain, has its own railway; there is an amusement arcade, donkey rides and a variety of evening entertainment. Boats can be hired on Marine Lake, where races and water-ski-ing demonstrations, including a twenty-four hour dinghy race, are held in summer, and bathers have a choice of sea, pool or saltwater swimming bath. For a bird's eye view of the town, take a pleasure flight from the airstrip near the esplanade.

On rainy days several museums keep boredom at bay, with collections of dolls, oil paintings and sculpture, relics of the shrimping industry and a model village. The Steamport Transport Museum promises to be the largest preservation centre in North West England. Already on show are mighty ex-British Rail locomotives and a standard gauge track, laid by museum members, connects the museum to the main rail system. Local buses, tramcars and traction engines, special events and steam days attract further interest.

A trip out of town to Martin Mere calls for a sunny day. The waterfowl garden covers forty acres with avaries, lakes and paddocks stocked with tame and flying wildfowl. A further 262 acres consists of wild marshland where many indigenous species live and breed as in the wild and are joined most winters by thousands of pink-footed geese. Visitors need not get wet feet themselves as hides are strategically placed for observation. The entrance building is also remarkable – a vast log cabin with a grass roof where geese graze freely.

Anglers can cast from the beach at Southport or along the estuary of the River Douglas for cod, dab, plaice and whiting, while offshore, a morning's fishing from a boat may intercept a shoal of bass, cod or mackerel. At

Tarleton, the leisure lakes are only used for boating, but sandy 'shores' are ideal for children and miles of woodland and heath attract picnickers and walkers.

For longer strolls, the desolate Forest of Bowland lies to the north of Preston. Like Exmoor, it is not really a forest at all; gone are the trees that were Royal hunting grounds, the expanses of peaty moorland support only cotton grass, wild broom and heather.

Preston is a bustling textiles, engineering and dock town and the birthplace of Sir Richard Arkwright, inventor of the Spinning Jenny, the cotton spinning machine which caused riots among millhands who feared automation and redundancy. The Harris Museum and Art Gallery contains archaeological and art treasures and prehistoric timbers from Bleasdale, and five miles to the east is the dramatic 16th-century hill-top mansion of Hoghton Tower.

This part of Lancashire reveals a variety of faces: unspoilt countryside studded with farms, villages and ancient market towns, sprawling industrial cities of brick and metal and a wild, remote coastline punctuated with fairy-light-hung resorts.

Things to do and see are equally diverse, in common with the choice of no less than ten golf courses in the Southport area and the intricacies of the Royal Birkdale itself.

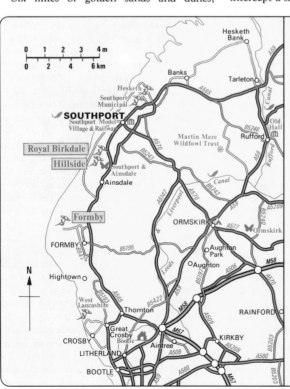

**Bootle**
*Tel: (051 928) 1371*
Urban course with some testing holes, 18 holes, 6282yds, par 68, SSS70
*Professional: F Lloyd*

**Hesketh (Southport)**
*Tel: (0704) 36897*
Breezy seaside course, 18 holes, 6498yds, par 71, SSS71
*Professional: J Donoghue*

**Ormskirk**
*Tel: (0695) 72112*
Quiet parkland course, 18 holes, 6327yds, par 70, SSS70
*Professional: A Kirby*

**Southport & Ainsdale**
*Tel: (0704) 78000*
Quality parkland course, 18 holes, 6574yds, par 72, SSS72
*Professional: I Murdoch*

**Southport Municipal**
*Tel: (0704) 35286*
Urban links course, 18 holes, 6139yds, par 70, SSS70
*Professionals: W & G Tomlinson*

**West Lancashire**
*Tel: (051 924) 1076*
Testing links course 4m N of Bootle off A565 at Crosby, 18 holes, 6694yds, par 72, SSS73
*Professional: D Lloyd*

**Angling**
Leeds & Liverpool Canal: fair coarse fishing with good access
Daily tickets: on bank or Wigan & District Angling Association (G A Chamberlain), 15 Frog Lane, Wigan
*Tel: (0942) 41932*
Water Authority: NWWA, New Town House, Buttermarket Street, Warrington
*Tel: (0925) 53999*
Rufford Canal: offshoot of Leeds & Liverpool Canal containing coarse fish
Daily tickets & Water Authority: as Leeds & Liverpool Canal
Southport: several good beach spots from Southport to Formby for cod, flounder, plaice & whiting. Plus bass, dogfish & mackerel by boat
Tackle shop: J E Robinson & Son, Sussex Road, Southport
*Tel: (0704) 34136*

**Camping**
Ormskirk: Abbey Farm Caravan Site ►►►
*Tel: (0695) 72686*
Secluded 39-pitch site (14 caravans)
Open all year, must book Jul–Aug

**General**
Aughton: Cranford: modern garden with rare shrubs & trees 3m SE of Ormskirk

Open Apr–mid-Oct daily 10–dusk
Bootle: Bootle Library: new library with painting & porcelain exhibits
Open Mon–Sat (Thu & Sat am only)
Ormskirk: Wildfowl Trust: large conservation area with many rare species 3m NE of Ormskirk off A59
Open all year daily 9.30–6.30 or dusk
*Tel: (0704) 895181*
Rufford: Rufford Old Hall: 17th & early 19th-century mansion with notable interior
Open Mar–Dec (ex Mon) 1–6, also closed Wed in Mar, Oct, Nov & Dec
Southport: Model Village & Model Railway: miniature community set within trees & shrubs
Open Mar–Oct 9–1hr before dusk
*Tel: (0704) 42133*
Southport Zoo: varied animal collection within pleasant 2½-acre grounds
Open all year daily 10–dusk
*Tel: (0704) 38102*
Steamport Transport Museum: locomotives, track plus numerous commercial vehicles, with steam-days every Sun in summer
Open Jun–mid-Sep daily 1–5 (weekends only in winter)
*Tel: (0704) 30693*

# Central &
# South Scotland

**5**

# Gullane and North Berwick

Gullane Golf Club, Gullane, East Lothian
*Tel: Gullane (0620) 842255*

North Berwick, Beach Road, North Berwick, East Lothian
*Tel: North Berwick (0620) 2135*

### Gullane

Off A198 coast road on edge of town about 17 miles from Edinburgh

Three seaside courses with a downland character. Course 1: 6444yds, SSS71; Course 2: 6090yds, SSS69; Course 3: 5012yds, SSS64

Visitors welcome, reservation advisable for Course 1
*Professional: J Hume*

### North Berwick

Off A198 7 miles further on from Gullane

Links course: 6317yds, SSS70

Visitors welcome: reservation advisable
*Professional: D Huish*

Hotels: Bissets★★ Gullane
*Tel: Gullane (0620) 842230*
(28 rm)

Greywalls★★★ (highly commended) Gullane
*Tel: Gullane (0620) 842144*
(20 rm)

Marine★★★ North Berwick
*Tel: North Berwick (0620) 2406*

Open Arms★★★ Dirleton
*Tel: Dirleton (062 085) 241*
(7 rm)

Gullane town is as near the heart of golfdom as you will ever find. Within the distance of a couple of hearty drives from the doorstep of the golf shop at the cross roads, you could be on five courses: Luffness New, the three splendid courses of the Gullane club and the famed

Muirfield. According to many, Jack Nicklaus among them, the latter is the best course by a short head and may even be the best test of golf in the world today.

Muirfield is not quite a links course in character, being the most inland of the five. Nor is it the best course for visiting golfers who want good golf, lovely scenery, a romantic tradition and no great heartaches at the end of a punishing round. Without beating around the bush, it is also almost impossible to get on this course, administered by the exclusively male Honourable Company of Edinburgh Golfers. For this reason, review of the delightful play to be had on this captivating Forth coast concentrates on the favoured Gullane No. 1 and another prime links location, but a few miles away, North Berwick.

Any visitor to this stretch of East Lothian coast should first take the hint that Gullane must *never* be pronounced Gull*ain*. The 'a' becomes a cross between a 'u' and an 'i' in local parlance so the correct rendition is something like 'Gullun'. Eighteen miles down the Firth of Forth from Scotland's magnificent capital,

Edinburgh, Gullane has one of the most inspiring views of all links courses. Of the three links laid out in this high foreshore, the No. 1 is incomparably the greatest – from the 7th tee you can see at least seven Scottish counties (before the incomprehensibility of the reorganisation!) and, on a clear day, the Ochil Hills. The panorama wanders over the coastline of the firth, Arthur's Seat, the twin bridges of the Forth and the purple sprawl of Edinburgh, large and magnificent. Also within view is the Bass Rock, sentinel light to the flock of shipping that is always in view, and way to the north are magnificent mountains.

Of the three courses at Gullane the Nos 2 and 3, respectively 6090 yards par 69 and 5012 yards par 65, are distinctly easier, by way of less demanding terrain and distances, than the 6444-yard No. 1. In fact they are popular for light-hearted family golf, something which the Gullane club positively encourages.

The first nine holes of Gullane 1, a course that attains considerable heights despite its links status, are probably the most enjoyable before you head downhill to the 12th and up

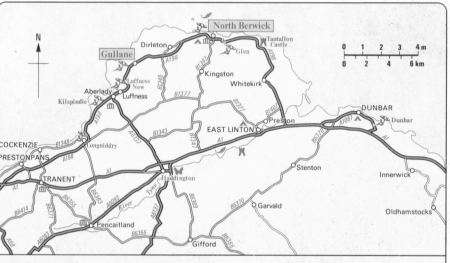

**Dunbar**
*Tel: (0368) 62317*
Old links course with natural hazards, 18 holes, 6407yds, par 71, SSS71
*Professional: W Paton*

**Glen**
*Tel: (0620) 2221*
Interesting seaside course 2m E of North Berwick off A198, 18 holes, 6079yds, par 69, SSS69
*Professional: D Huish*

**Haddington**
*Tel: (062 082) 3627*
Easily walked parkland course. 18 holes, 5997yds, par 70, SSS69

**Kilspindie**
*Tel: (087 57) 216*
Short, but testing seaside course 3m SW of Gullane at Aberlady, 18 holes, 5423yds, par 69, SSS66

**Longniddry**
*Tel: (0875) 52141*
Good links course 5m E of Prestonpans, 18 holes, 6240yds, par 68, SSS70
*Professional: J Durward*

**Luffness New**
*Tel: (0620) 843114*
Links course 3m S of Gullane off A198, 18 holes, 6085yds, par 70, SSS69

**WEST LINKS COURSE, NORTH BERWICK**

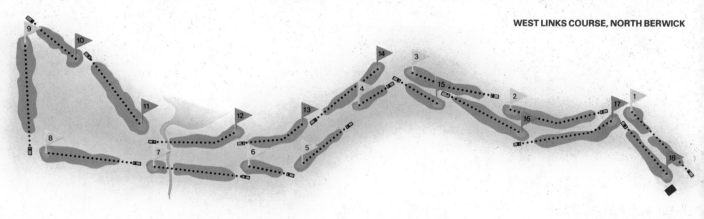

*North Berwick*

**Angling**
North Berwick: shore fishing to Dunbar, plus by boat for cod, haddock, mackerel & plaice
Tackle shop: Wilco Sports & Engineering, Tantallon Road, North Berwick
*Tel: (0620) 3686*
River Tyne: fair trout, but still recovering from effects of pollution
Daily tickets: North Berwick Angling Club (G B Woodburn), 29 Craigleith Avenue, North Berwick
*Tel: (0620) 3120*

**Camping**
Dunbar: Kirk Park Caravan Site ►►
Partly sloping 21-pitch site
Open mid-Mar–Oct, no bookings
Winterfield Caravan Site ►►
Grassy 19-pitch site
Open Apr–Sep, no bookings
East Linton: Monksmuir Caravan Park ►►
*Tel: (062 086) 340*
Fairly level 43-pitch site (20 tents)
Open Apr–Sep, no bookings
North Berwick: Rhodes Caravan Site ►►
Level 350-pitch site near sea
Open mid-Mar–Sep, no bookings

**General**
Aberlady: Myreton Motor Museum:

large motor-cycle, car & military vehicle collection
Open Easter–Oct daily 10–6 (Sat & Sun only in winter)
*Tel: (087 57) 288*
East Linton: Hailes Castle: ancient fortified manor with 16th-century chapel
Open all year
Preston Mill: rare working water-mill
Open all year
Mon–Sat 10–12.30 & 2–7 (until 4.30 in winter)
North Berwick: Museum of Flight: early airship base, now houses display of aircraft & rockets, 5m S of Berwick at East Fortune Airfield
Open Jul–Aug daily 10–4
*Tel: (031 225) 7534*
Tantallon Castle: 14th-century fortress 3m E of North Berwick
Open all year
Pencaitland: Winton House: 17th-century mansion with later additions, beautifully furnished
Open to parties by appointment
*Tel: (0875) 349222*
Tranent: Prestongrange Historical Site & Mining Museum: 800-year-old coal-mining site, two colliery locomotives (active on steam days) & exhibition hall
Open Mon–Fri 9–4.30 (Sat by appointment)
*Tel: (031 661) 2718*

again across the 13th for three more holes until the hill is recrossed again for the 18th. All the holes are on fine turf occasionally sheltered from winds – although where the view is the best you are particularly exposed to winds whipping across the estuary.

The first tee is almost literally in the village, just a few yards from the High Street. You will have to take care on the way back, too. The 18th is a middle-distance 355-yard par 4 on which it is easy to end up in the shops as long-hitting Dutch professional Roesink found in an Open qualifier. He drove straight through the green with a 4-wood well on the way to landing in a shopping basket. The course record is registered by an amateur, Joe Carr, with 64, which is a superb card on this par 71 course.

Driving east from Gullane you quickly reach the most photogenic of these ancient golfing strongholds. North Berwick is never used these days for major championships – a great loss to the game which has been brought about by the ever-increasing necessity to accommodate large crowds of spectators. Dotted in the sea off this links are picturesque islets – Fidra, The Lamb, Craigleith and others dwarfed by the great Bass Rock and all lively with bird populations of which the gannet is the most raucous.

Old caddies used to instruct their patrons, 'Take a line on the rock, sir, and remember Bass is good for you'. Next to St Andrews, North Berwick is the butt of good golf stories. It is a links that is known across the world, particularly in the Americas for its excellent 15th. A par 3, 'Redan' has been copied on

some of the best courses in the USA and even in South America.

North Berwick is a traditionally designed straight-out, straight-in links with eight holes that border the beach. The 1st is regarded as a terrifying opener, with seasonal holidaymakers being as great a hazard as its cruel sandpit. A good straight drive is required at the second, a successful over-the-wall shot has to be played at the 3rd and you are away across the rolling ground. This wall comes into play considerably on this course (known as the West Course) and there is the Eil Burn to negotiate at the 7th and 12th. From the 14th, the course has a classic ending. There is the famous 190-yard 'Redan' and 'Point Garry', the 17th, which shares its fairway with that of the 1st. Among the barbed hole names at North Berwick are many nautical references: 'Sea', 'Linkhouse', 'Mizzentop', 'Eastward Ho!' and 'Bosun's Locker'.

The whole of the coast from Gullane round almost to North Berwick has been severely threatened by erosion. Windblown sands threatened the original 12th-century settlement in the 17th-century so badly that by Act of Parliament a new church was erected at Dirleton, two and a half miles away on less threatened ground. This is land that is now forested and walkers can enjoy the nature trail laid out over interesting geological features, woodlands and seashore. Nearby, in Aberlady, there is a bird sanctuary and nature reserve for the thousands of seabirds that inhabit this fascinating coastline. Most of this coastline can be walked provided care is taken to avoid the areas marked for restoration of sea defences

by the plantation of marram grass and some dune reinforcements.

North Berwick is the sea angling centre of the area with good boat fishing out of the port for cod, haddock, mackerel, and coalfish. At low water, baits are available on the shore. Better shore fishing is available further east towards Dunbar, a town claiming the lowest rainfall in the whole of Scotland (and more sunshine). North Berwick, on the other hand, has the better bathing beaches of this coast and most of the facilities of a small seaside resort including a popular, and large, campsite.

One of the more charming features of both Gullane and the North Berwick is the lengths to which both clubs go to encourage younger golfers. At Gullane they have their very own 5-hole children's course, while North Berwick has a 9-hole for juniors as well as an annual children's tournament.

For youngsters under fifteen, the tournament is for a fine medal which can be inspected, among many other golf memorabilia, at the clubhouse. In 1882, when the children only played 12 holes, the winner was an English lad with a score card of 95. More recently, a 14-year-old returned a 75 net after a 5 handicap over the full eighteen – visiting players should look to their laurels!

# Royal Troon

Royal Troon, Craigend Road,
Troon, Ayrshire
*Tel: Troon (0292) 311555*

Off B749 3 miles from Prestwick
Airport

Two seaside links: Old Course: 6649yds,
SSS73; Portland Course: 6274yds,
SSS70
Design modified by James Braid
Visitors welcome, reservation advisable
Old course, visitors after 9.30am
*Professional:* R Anderson

Hotels: Craiglea★★ South Beach
*Tel: Troon (0292) 311366*
(22 rm)

Marine★★★★ Troon
*Tel: Troon (0292) 314444*
(68 rm)

South Beach★★ South Beach
*Tel: Troon (0292) 312033*
(25 rm)

If ever proof were needed that Scotland is golf-mad, it is to be found on the resort coast of Ayrshire in the ten miles of coast between Ayr itself and Irvine. On this seaside playground of Scotland's industrial south there are no less than eleven golf clubs, boasting between them fifteen links courses. Among this galaxy of golf for the touring player, the focus is Royal Troon's Old Course, a stretch of sandy heath that has probably incurred more vilification by some of the world's greatest golfers than any other venue of the Open.

'Nobody told me they'd fought a war here' commented Gay Brewer; 'The British Open course is like a zoo', cried Bob Rosburg. Bitterly reviewing the club's motto *'Tam arte quam morte'* (More skill than strength), Jack Nicklaus muttered 'You can say that again' after his less-than-sparkling first-round 80 in the 1962 Open at Troon.

What arouses the ire of the famous is a set of humps and hollows on ground that at first appears to be flat and unremarkable. There are gradients on the fairways and vicious winds that either follow you out or remain to catch you on the return. Further problems are caused by hidden greens on the 9th and 15th.

Old Troon has hosted Open Championships which have made history. The first, in 1923, produced an English winner in Arthur Havers at the time of a 12-year American ascendancy. This was the tournament in which the young Gene Sarazen failed to qualify – fifty years later in the same event he hit a hole in one at the 'Postage Stamp' 8th. Often described as the stamp that licks the player, this is the hole on which German amateur Herman Tissies took fifteen strokes during an Open; it is the shor-

test par 3 of any Open course, a 123-yard par 3.

Troon's club has been in existence since 1878 but it was not until 1909 that a course comparable to the present design was laid out by the incumbent professional Willie Fernie. Even then the 8th was a formidable short hole which occasioned a club council minute to the effect that members were concerned about its fairness and 'The green is extremely small and it is a most difficult matter to get the ball to stay on it.' In 1923 James Braid suggested additional bunkers to the left of the green making today's perplexing hazards.

As well as the shortest hole, Troon also boasts the longest Open challenge, the 580-yard 6th. It is a long bounding dogleg to the right on a line through guard bunkers, a route that now avoids the deep drop which so confounded early Open players to the left of the green approach. Among Troon's few holes where a straight drive will go some way towards the green, is the revised 11th. A dogleg in the original design, a new tee almost completely straightened the fairway, which was narrowed down by allowing the rough to encroach considerably further into the left hand side.

Troon's roughs should never be ignored. While in many places they prevent your ball getting into even deeper trouble among the gorse bushes which throng the linksland, they do constrict the fairways to a noticeable extent and call for very accurate driving. Two elderly Canadian businessmen, who flew over to the nearby Prestwick airport and spent a long weekend playing 'six heavenly rounds' at Troon, also admitted to the loss of 34 balls between them.

Visitors be warned, the clubhouse at Old Troon is a holy of holies for the exclusive use of male members and their guests – the adjoining Portland Club and its associated 6274-yard par 70 course is the ladies' club (the course can be played by both sexes). On both courses permission to play is readily granted to visitors and with a little persuasion, male visiting golfers will be allowed in the Royal Troon clubhouse. The building is garnished with interesting relics. On exhibition is what is claimed to be the oldest known set of golf clubs. Discovered when an old building in Hull was demolished, the clubs belonged to one Stuart king over 300 years ago. The hafts, made of ash, are still in good condition and unwarped.

The town of Troon faces the wide waters of the Firth of Clyde with distant views of the mountainous Isle of Arran. While golf is probably the main attraction, the Troon beaches offer good bathing and there is a sprinkling of the usual resort facilities. The long arm of the harbour, part of the town's jutting promontory, is a favourite sea angling spot and cod and flatfish abound from the Barassie sands. Boat trips run from the harbour to the bird sanctuary of Lady Isle and there are also charter boats available for fishing trips to the many wreck marks in the surrounding seas.

However, as a resort it is Ayr, some eight miles south of Troon, that is the greater attraction. Here is all the fun of the seaside with ponies on the sands, paddling and swimming pools, miniature golf, a fairground and tennis

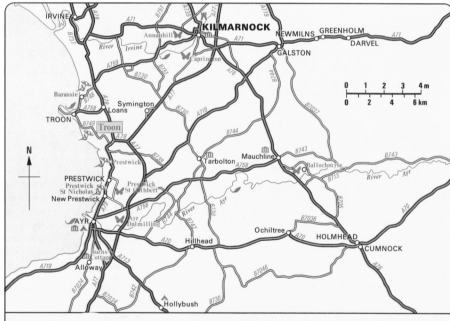

**Annanhill**
*Tel: (0563) 21644*
Parkland course 2m W of
Kilmarnock, 18 holes, 6269yds,
par 71, SSS70
*Professional:* W Fraser

**Ayr Dalmilling (Ayr)**
*Tel: (0292) 63893*
Easily walked meadowland
course, 18 holes, 5300yds, par
67, SSS66
*Professional:* D McKay

**Ballochmyle**
*Tel: (0290) 50469*

Parkland course 2m NE of
Mauchline off A76, 18 holes,
5847yds, par 70, SSS69

**Barassie (Kilmarnock)**
*Tel: (0563) 311077*
Very good seaside course 2m N
of Troon, 18 holes, 6435yds, par
71, SSS71
*Professional:* W Lockie

**Caprington (Kilmarnock)**
*Tel: (0563) 21915*
Urban parkland course, 18 holes,
5951yds, par 69, SSS69
*Professional:* W Fraser

**Prestwick**
*Tel: (0292) 77404*
Links course, 18 holes, 6544yds,
par 71, SSS72
*Professional:* F Rennie

**Prestwick St Cuthbert**
*Tel: (0292) 77107*
Easily walked parkland course, 18
holes, 6349yds, par 71, SSS70

**Prestwick St Nicholas**
*Tel: (0292) 77608*
Windy seaside course, 18 holes,
5809yds, par 69, SSS68
*Professional:* W MacDonald

**OLD COURSE**

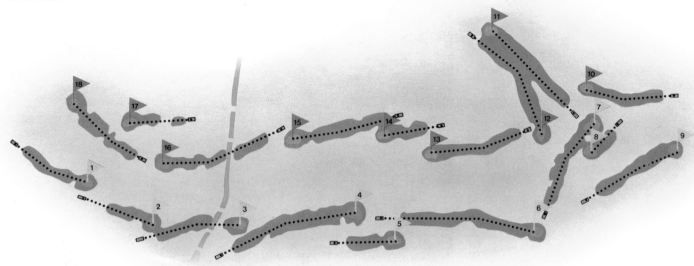

courts. The River Ayr can be fished for sea trout, salmon, and brown trout in season and sea anglers can expect cod, dogfish, flounders and haddock taken from charter boats and from popular shore marks. The Firth of Clyde is a great sailing area and small boats can be launched from Ayr with other yachting facilities at nearby Prestwick and, north of Troon, at Irvine. For walkers, the Rozelle nature trail lies south of the town. A fascinating walk, the trail illustrates plant and animal life in ponds and natural woodlands.

For those visitors interested in history, Ayr, Troon and Kilmarnock all have Burns links. Ayr has the Tam o' Shanter Museum housed in a building in which the poet used to drink and Burns Cottage where he lived. Kilmarnock was where the first edition of his poems was published and a town in which he hoped to raise

the money to settle in Jamaica. It was the success of his poems that deterred him from emigration. The town, an industrial centre, is also the home of the Johnny Walker whisky company – the original Johnny Walker was a grocer in King Street who began to blend various whiskies to achieve uniform quality. This distiller is now the largest whisky-maker in the world and exports are thriving.

The sandy beaches of Ayr stretch all the way past Troon to Irvine, yet another settling place of the peripatetic Burns. The town is a Royal burgh and port at the meeting of River Irvine and Annick Water and it is here that Alfred Nobel sited one of the first of his factories to produce the dynamite that made him his fortune – now handed down to scientists, writers and philanthropists as the Nobel Prizes. Irvine is a centre for both pony-trekking and sailing

and also offers fresh and saltwater fishing.

It is, of course, this enormous length of sandy foreshore that has given rise to the very many links along this coast. Only a few miles from Prestwick's airport or an hour or so by road from Glasgow, the marvels of the Troon course are among the most accessible of Scotland's golfing jewels.

**Angling**
Ayr: harbour fishing for cod, dab, dogfish & flounder. Boat fishing may add haddock, pollack & whiting
River Ayr: fair salmon plus trout & grayling
Daily tickets (in advance): Kyle & District Council, Town Buildings, Ayr
*Tel: (0292) 81511.*
River Irvine: quality trout with very good access
Daily tickets: McCririck & Sons, 39 John Finnie Street, Kilmarnock
*Tel: (0563) 25577*
Troon: good shore fishing for coalfish, cod, plaice & pollack. Plus gurnard & tope by boat

**Camping**
Ayr: Trax Campsite ►►► Grassy 250-pitch site near sea
Open early Apr then mid-May–mid-Sep (ex 10–12, 18–22 Jul & 4–6 Aug), no bookings
Hollybush: Skeldon Caravans ►►
*Tel: (029 256) 202*
Quiet 30-pitch site 6m SE of Ayr off B7034
Open Apr–Sep, must book Jul–Aug
Kilmarnock: Cunninghead Head Estate Caravan Park ►
*Tel: (029 485) 238*
Small 80-pitch site (40 tents) 5m NW of Kilmarnock off B769
Open Apr–Sep, no bookings

**Riding**
Ayr: Ayrshire Equitation Centre (J A Gilbraith), Castlehills Stables, Hillfoot Road, Ayr
*Tel: (0292) 66267*

**General**
Alloway: Burns Cottage: birthplace of Robert Burns, now museum
Open Apr–mid-Oct daily 9–7 (Sun 2–7, 11–7 Jun, Jul & Aug)
Ayr: Tam O'Shanter Museum: believed starting point of Tam O'Shanter's ride, now houses Robert Burns items
Open Apr–Sep Mon–Sat 9.30–5.30 (12–4 in winter), also Sun Jun, Jul & Aug
Irvine: Eglinton Castle & Gardens: 18th-century fortress set in 12-acre grounds
Open all year
*Tel: (0294) 74166*
Kilmarnock: Burns Museum: extensive collection of the poet's works
Open May–Sep daily 1–5 (Sat & Sun only in winter)
*Tel: (0563) 26401*
Dean Castle: 14th-century fortified tower housing armour & musical instrument exhibits
Open mid-May–mid-Sep (Mon–Fri afternoons only)
*Tel: (0563) 26401*
Tarbolton: Bachelors' Club: 17th-century house, former Burns' society HQ
Open Apr–Sep daily 10–6

# Gleneagles Hotel

Gleneagles Hotel
Auchterarder, Tayside
*Tel: Auchterarder (076 46) 2231*
*Telex: 76105*

Three moorland courses: King's
6503yds, SSS71,
Queen's 6278yds, SSS70, Prince's
('Wee') 5128yds, SSS65
*Course designer:* James Braid

Visitors welcome – reservation
advisable (open 10am)
*Professional: I Marchbank*

Hotels: Gleneagles Hotel ★★★★★
(189rm) closed November – mid-April
Ruthven Tower ★★ Abbey Road,
Auchterarder
*Tel: (076 46) 2578*
(10rm – annexe 8rm)
Blackford ★★ Moray Street, Blackford
*Tel: (076 482) 246*
(6rm)

From the imposing heights of Stirling Castle to
the first folds of the countryside heralding the
majestic rise of the Highlands, the approach to
Gleneagles along the A9 is as exhilarating as
the setting of this premier hotel and golf course
itself. Over 700 acres of spectacular moorland
rise and fall around a magnificently appointed
building designed in a style that recalls the
splendour of watering holes along the European Grand Tour. Yet this course, arguably
one of the finest works of Veteran Open
Championship winner James Braid, is only
sixty years old.

Three courses, with a fourth nearly completed, comprise this golfing jewel. The best
views are to be seen from the elevated tees of
the 6278-yard Queen's Course, originally a
9-hole. For this is the head of Strathallan, a
great split in the Tayside hills and a meeting
place of valleys which include the nearby Glen
Eagles itself. For the faint at heart there are the
less rigorous fairways of the Prince's Course,
once dismissively known as the 'Wee' course
and very much the province of the ladies, with
its many short drives.

The glory of Gleneagles, trod with awe by
visitors, celebrities and professionals alike, is
the King's Course, 6503 yards of doglegs and
subtle traps made all the more difficult by the
deceptively tumbling and soaring topography.
Almost every green, detailed by that fastidious
father of Gleneagles, Donald Matheson, forms
its own natural amphitheatre, a delight for the
spectators of the many regular Double
Diamond and Pro-Celebrity events held here.

Deception begins with the wide, inviting

**KING'S COURSE**

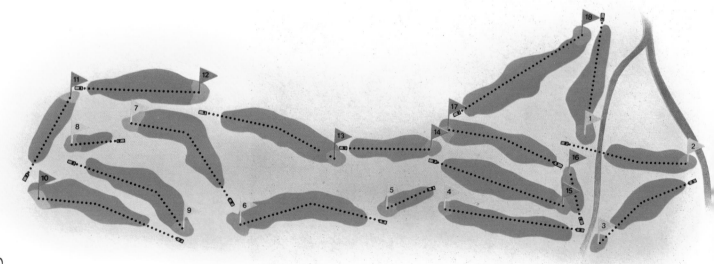

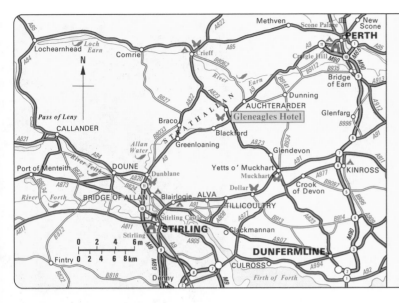

**Craigie Hill**
*Tel: Perth (0738) 24377*
Park course on western suburbs
of Perth by A9 Glasgow road
*Designer:* J Anderson
18 holes, 5288yds, SSS66
Visitors welcome, prior call
necessary at weekends

**Crieff**
*Tel: Crieff (0764) 2909*
Undulating parkland course on
A85 2m NE of Crieff.
*Designer:* James Braid
18 holes, 5901yds, SSS68
Visitors welcome, reservation
necessary
*Professional:* J Stark

**Dollar**
*Tel: Dollar (025 94) 2400*
Course on hillside 13m E of
Stirling ½m N of A91
18 holes, 4960yds, SSS65
Visitors welcome at weekends
with members only

**Dunblane**
*Tel: Dunblane (0786) 822343*
Park course close to A9 in
Dunblane (t. rt at Fourways
Restaurant rbt)
18 holes, 5874yds, SSS68
Visitors welcome weekdays only

**Muckhart**
*Tel: Muckhart (025 981) 420*
Moorland course by A91 17m E of
Stirling
18 holes, 6095yds, SSS70
Visitors welcome after 10am at
weekends
*Professional:* S Glass

**Stirling**
*Tel: Stirling (0786) 3801*
Undulating Kings Park course on
south side of A811 ½m W of
Stirling town centre
*Designer:* Tom Morris
18 holes, 6438yds, SSS71
Visitors welcome on weekdays
and Sunday pm

fairway of hole one – 'Dun Whinny', named, like all the holes, by Matheson exercising his dour humour. The green is a high plateau some 360 yards away – so high, in fact, that it foreshortens the strength of many a player's second shot, luring the ball into a gaping trap at the foot of the slope. After only 200 yards or so of the second hole, 'East Neuk', the fairway narrows to a funnel through gorse and bracken which makes the tee shot of utmost importance. These two bits of trickery should amply prepare you for the split-level green of 'Silver Tassie'. Loft the ball high over the ridge with a game second shot and you still cannot afford to relax with only two putts in hand.

Anything but accurate straight drives on the 465-yard 4th ('Broomey Law') lands you in sand or heather and a fine preparation for the devilishly short 5th, 'Het Girdle', on which there is no room for less than pinpoint precision. Bunkers are to the front and right of the green – to the left is a precipitous slope. Two long doglegs on the 6th and 7th and you are faced with another single-shot hole – the 170-yard 'Whaup's Nest', featuring a catch-all bunker almost dead in front of the green.

No fewer than four holes on the return exceed 450 yards, so you will be heavily reliant on fair winds that paradoxically present their greatest threat on the short (233-yard) 11th, 'Deil's Creel'. Hole 12 'Tappit Hen' is the softener for 13, 'Braid's Brawest'; a daunting 451 yards which starts with a ridge guarded by two bunkers. If you make this with one shot you have a second to make on to the green plateau, with bunkers to the front and left. Putting is a heartfelt relief. You may be able to pick up a stroke on the often downwind 14th with its sentinels of bracken and gorse, but prepare yourself for the teasing two-tier green of the 15th, 'Howe o' Hope' after straight drives totalling 460 yards. 'Wee Bogle' at 16 is the shortest of all – 135 yards over a bath of sand on to a green like a postage stamp, with bunker perforations. The modest length of 17 belies its mean dogleg, demanding a second shot accuracy that some believe is the most testing stroke at Gleneagles. And for the not-so-fit, a par 5 on the glorious 531-yard 'King's

Hame' may seem the final injury. The 18th green itself, where fortunes and composure are won and lost many times a year, is a monster to rob you of at least two strokes.

Few will visit this region of Scotland, a natural and historic gateway to the Highlands, for the golf alone. Stirling and Tayside, hold many tourist attractions.

Stirling Castle dominating the centre of the town, has many 13th-century structures, although fortifications on this rock overlooking the Forth go back to pre-Roman times. The castle's most striking features are the comparatively modern 16th-century additions in a Renaissance style. Stirling was a favourite of Queen Victoria's, and her lookout point and the nearby Ladies' Rock provide superb views of the town and surrounding countryside. Within the castle is the palace of King James V, which today houses the regimental museum of the Argyll and Sutherland Highlanders, tracing their history from Waterloo to the present day. A modern multi-screen slide and film presentation of the castle's history is shown daily in the Landmark Visitor's Centre which also contains a small theatre and shops full of local souvenirs.

Tayside vies with the Spey for the title of top Scottish game fishing area. It once yielded a 64lb salmon to a lady angler (in 1922!) which stands as today's British record. While much of the finer game fishing is in the more northerly parts of the river (and tributaries such as the Tummel), the River Earn, flowing close to Gleneagles and entering the Tay nine miles south east of Perth, has its share of the system's salmon run and a good stock of trout. Tickets for seven miles of the river around Crieff are available from W Cook & Sons, 19 High Street, Crieff.

Nearby Auchterarder is the home of the Strathallan Aircraft Collection. Collected from all over the world, this static display includes such landmarks in aviation history as the Tiger Moth, World War II aircraft such as the Hurricane, Mosquito and Lancaster and curiosities like the Anson, Harvard and Hudson. The collection is open from 10am–5pm (or dusk in winter).

**Angling**
Allan Water:
Dunblane – Forth
junction
Day tickets from
Crockart & Son,
Stirling or Allanbank
Hotel, Greenloaning
trout, salmon
River Earn: 9m
around Crieff
Daily tickets: W Cook
& Sons, 19 High
Street, Crieff
*Tel: (0764) 2081*
Gleneagles Hotel
grounds:
Day tickets from
Head Hall Porter
(residents only), trout
River Teith: Callander
– Forth junction
Day tickets from
riparian owners and
bailiffs – public
stretches, Stirling
District Council,
Municipal Buildings,
Stirling, trout,
salmon, sea trout
Upper & Lower:
Glendevon
Reservoirs: 5m NW
of Dollar, limited boat
fishing
Day tickets from Mrs
J Main, Waterman's
House (at reservoirs)
or in advance from
Water Division, Fife
Regional Council,
Craig Mitchell House,
Glenrothes, trout

**Camping**
Blairlogie: Witches
Craig Farm Camping
and
Caravan Park►►
*Tel: Stirling 4947*
Small site on A91 3m
NE of town centre
with 60 pitches
Open Apr–Sep
Bridge of Allan: Allan
Water
Caravan Site►►►
Blairforkie Drive
*Tel: (0786) 832254*
Small caravans only,
site on banks of Allan
with 50 pitches
Open Apr–Sep
Comrie: Twenty
Shilling Wood
Caravan Site►►►
*Tel: (076 47) 411*
Quiet 30-pitch site

(no tents) 7m W
Crieff
Open Apr–Sep, no
bookings
Crieff: Crieff Holiday
Village►►►
*Tel: (0764) 3513*
1m W of Crieff on
A85, set in woodland
with 38 pitches. Boat
hire and fishing on
Earn
Open Mar–Dec
Kinross: Loch Leven
Caravan Site►►►
*Tel: (0577) 63560*
Small 36-pitch site on
shores of Loch with
good views and
some seclusion.
Open Apr–Sep

**General**
Auchterarder:
Strathallan Aircraft
Collection:
impressive display of
many vintage aircraft
Open all year 10–5 (or
dusk in winter)
*Tel: (076 46) 2545*
Crieff: Innerpeffray
Library: 2nd oldest
library in Scotland.
Open all year (ex
Thur)
*Tel: (0764) 2819*
Dunblane: Keir:
lovely rhododendron,
shrub & water
gardens
Open Apr – Oct Tue,
Wed & Thu
*Tel: (0786) 822200*
Muthill: Drummond
Castle Gardens:
beautiful Trust
gardens 4m S of
Crieff
Open Apr–Sep 2–6
(Wed & Sun only)
*Tel: (076 481) 257*
Perth: Black Watch
Regimental
Museum: numerous
items of 42nd/73rd
Highland regiment.
Open all year
*Tel: (0738) 26287*
Fair Maid's House:
over 600-year-old
building with many
historic connections,
now a crafts &
antiques centre
Open all year 10–5
(ex Sun)
*Tel: (0738) 25976*

# St Andrews, Carnoustie and Blairgowrie

St Andrews Links Management
Committee, Golf Place,
St Andrews, Fife
*Tel: St Andrews (0334) 74637 (Old
Course starter (0334 81) 3393)*

Carnoustie, Links Parade,
Carnoustie, Angus
*Tel: Carnoustie (0241) 53249*

Blairgowrie, Rosemount,
Blairgowrie, Perthshire, Tayside
*Tel: Blairgowrie (0250) 2622*

---

St Andrews

Courses are to the north of the A91 a
mile before entering the town

Four fine seaside links:
Old Course: 6581yds, SSS71
New Course: 6524yds, SSS71
Eden Course: 5976yds, SSS69
Jubilee Course: 5938yds, SSS68

Visitors welcome, reservations at least 8
weeks in advance advisable
Daily ballot for play on Old Course

Carnoustie

On A930 coast road about 1 mile west of
Carnoustie

Two seaside courses: Championship:
6804yds, SSS74; Burnside: 5935yds,
SSS69

Visitors welcome, reservation advisable

Blairgowrie

On A93 15 miles north of Perth

Two heathland courses of 6592yds,
SSS72 and 6621yds, SSS72

Visitors welcome, reservation essential
*Professional:* G Kinnoch

Hotels: Angus★★ Blairgowrie
*Tel: Blairgowrie (0250) 2838*
(70 rm)

Bruce★★★ Carnoustie
*Tel: Carnoustie (0241) 52364*
(36 rm)

Glencoe★★ Carnoustie
*Tel: Carnoustie (0241) 53273*
(11 rm)

Old Course★★★★ St Andrews
*Tel: (033 481) 74371*
(68 rm)

Rufflets★★★ St Andrews
*Tel: St Andrews (033 481) 72594*
(19 rm)

---

St Andrews, with an age-long obsession for
golf that saved this former ecclesiastical capital
from obscurity, is also a fine Scottish family
holiday resort. Glorious sandy beaches and an
attractive harbour will while away many an
hour for the group robbed of its golf fanatics by
the proximity of *four* superb links courses en-
twined with a tradition that amounts to relig-
ion. The Old, the New (nearly a century old!),
the Eden and the Jubilee, comprise a Mecca to
the world's golfers. If that was not enough, this
pearl, close to the game fishing delights of the
Tay, is also complemented by the nearby
heavens of Carnoustie and Blairgowrie's
Rosemount Course. Here we attempt to com-
pare this trilogy of Scottish courses.

At St Andrews, the great championship
terrain is the Old, a playground that has with-
stood more praise and curses than any in the
world, not excluding the Colosseum in Rome.
The golf traffic is therefore considerable and
the greenkeeper's moan is that on any day in
midsummer he could pick up a whole coffin
full of divots.

In fact this old links, with its first tee be-
neath the terrifying window of the Royal and
Ancient clubhouse, dominates St Andrews.
Bobby Jones called it 'golf's examination paper'

**OLD COURSE, ST ANDREWS**

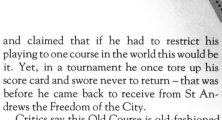

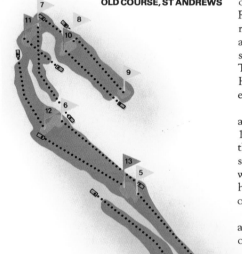

and claimed that if he had to restrict his
playing to one course in the world this would be
it. Yet, in a tournament he once tore up his
score card and swore never to return – that was
before he came back to receive from St Andrews the Freedom of the City.

Critics say this Old Course is old-fashioned
and they have a point. Nature determined its
characteristics and these have changed but
little over the years. An American Open
champion once declared 'twenty bulldozers
could make this dump fit for golf' – but that was
after the links had soundly whipped him.

---

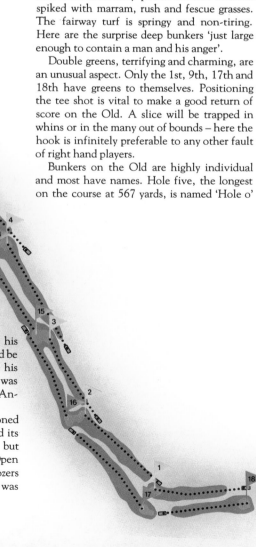

*St Andrews*

It is a traditional, flat, sea heath; seven holes
out, a loop by the game angler's delight of the
River Eden, and then seven home. Gently
rolling fairways have knolls here and there,
and some tortuously placed shallow hollows
spiked with marram, rush and fescue grasses.
The fairway turf is springy and non-tiring.
Here are the surprise deep bunkers 'just large
enough to contain a man and his anger'.

Double greens, terrifying and charming, are
an unusual aspect. Only the 1st, 9th, 17th and
18th have greens to themselves. Positioning
the tee shot is vital to make a good return of
score on the Old. A slice will be trapped in
whins or in the many out of bounds – here the
hook is infinitely preferable to any other fault
of right hand players.

Bunkers on the Old are highly individual
and most have names. Hole five, the longest
on the course at 567 yards, is named 'Hole o'

BURNSIDE COURSE, CARNOUSTIE

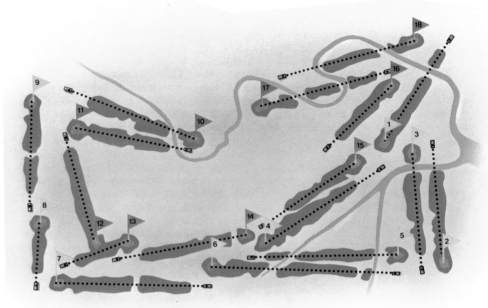

Cross' and has eight traps called Ginger Beer, Grave, Hell, Kitchen, Benty, Elysian Fields, Beardies and Pulpit. Problems aplenty of course, and what you would expect at this seat of golf – yet Peter Alliss returned a 66 and Neil Coles holds the course record with a fine 65.

Golfers will always remember a first visit to St Andrews, which is a round that should be accompanied by a caddie to savour the full delights. He will show you how to play the hole (and how to play!) and will regale you with the Old's many legends. How that colourful character Andrew Kirkaldy, caddying for the Prince of Wales, held up his clubs and asked 'When are you going to get rid of these auld shinty sticks?'. You will learn how Bing Crosby sat on the hallowed steps of the R and A crooning White Christmas to a crowd of locals and how another infamous caddy gave a putting lesson to Gary Middlecoff on the carpet of Rusack's Hotel. . . .

The main hotel at St Andrews is now called The Old Course. Overlooking the 17th hole, it stands on the site of old railway sheds famous for the fact that confident players would try to drive over the roofs in attempting a short cut to the hole. This is a luxurious four-star, British Transport Hotel, but for cannier players there is a good choice of less illustrious establishments in a town from which one never really escapes golf. When rain threatens the main shopping streets, it is the brightly coloured golf umbrella that dominates the scene. By the ancient church, a statue of local hero young Tom Morris takes a golfing stance.

To the visiting player, certain drolleries soon become apparent. For example, there is no general clubhouse where the usual facilities are granted to all who have paid their green fees. This temple overlooking the first tee is the regal sanctum of the Royal and Ancient, benevolent (some say) ruler of British golf. Members can entertain friends there, but an

unannounced entry is not on. Bob Hope and a friend once enquired of the uniformed janitor where they might change their clothes and were coolly told that uninvited golfers usually change in their cars.

Remember that to play the Old you book a day in advance, stipulating the time you wish to play and your name is put in a draw. If you are lucky, your name will be on the starting list displayed prominently at the club's Starter's Box (where the green fee is paid) and two or three other locations around the town. It is these minor inconveniences that make St Andrews golf that bit more precious.

Exactly fifteen miles away to the north of St Andrews, as a gull would fly over the Tay estuary, Carnoustie stretches out her 7000 yards of tiger golf. Players will have to take a car ride round the fine Dundee bridge road to reach the course within an hour.

Carnoustie boasts two links – the Championship Course and the shorter Burnside. While St Andrews basks in the romantic traditions of golf history, Carnoustie is the pragmatic one, long, mean and tough. Tommy Armour, Henry Cotton, Ben Hogan and Tom Watson (after a tie) won their Opens here and all declared afterwards that the victories had been supreme struggles.

The Carnoustie Burnside links, seemingly flat, has exciting features. Two tortuous burns twist about the course like angry serpents. The Barry must be crossed seven times, so any reputation the links might have as a slogger's paradise are swiftly dispelled. Bunkers are sited to trap powerful players rather than the visitor long on handicap. No two holes are similar and fairways seldom run parallel, so one's sense of wind direction comes into play more often than on most courses.

Some of the first few holes enjoy welcome shelter from a plantation of fir trees but then comes the double dogleg of hole six and any consolation from the shelter immediately vanishes. The short 8th hole is the first par 3 and the two further short holes in the home run of nine are no easier than this boundary hole. Curiously, hole sixteen is called 'Barry Burn'. The course's finest short hole is barely intruded upon by the stream, as this is a once on to the green hole if ever there was one. It is seventeen, played across a loop of the burn that uses the hazard to its best advantage.

As is usual with Scottish courses, all holes have appropriate names. The 10th is 'South America', because a Carnoustie worthy once planned to go there but could not withstand his farewell party. He awoke near this very hole and found he had no inclination to travel any further.

'Would the club consider issuing members with steel helmets as protection against the fusillade of rifle fire at hole six?', rates as one of the more curious requests ever put before Carnoustie's council, the club's ruling body. Rebellious member Torrington Bell was protesting against the enthusiastic overshoot of cadets on a firing range adjacent to this long hole and the club did eventually put an end to this unnecessary hazard.

By the Starter's Box there is a plaque naming those of Carnoustie's sons who have gone afar and conquered. Bobby Jones always claimed a 'Carnoustie swing' because he learnt much from Stewart Maiden who went to the States spreading the gospel he learnt in Scotland.

About thirty miles west of Carnoustie one discovers a course that is reckoned among the best inland Scottish locations. To be sure it cannot rival Gleneagles, but the golf at Blairgowrie Golf Club, Rosemount, is splendid in a Sunningdale sort of way – a course of parasol pines, silver birches and sylvan glades. James Braid remodelled the course in 1934 but the early golf terrain went back to 1889 when nine holes were hewn from forest land on the Marquess of Lansdowne's estate. The Marquess charged the club just ten shillings a year.

Because trees line Rosemount's avenue fairways there is an agreeable privacy about each hole; different indeed from the open aspects of St Andrews and Carnoustie. Many holes are

dogleg and the turf is so good that on long holes like the 14th you can use a driver from the fairway.

Blairgowrie's club has not named all the holes, but the 16th is referred to as 'Black Loch'. A stretch of water of Wagnerian gloom threatens on the habitual hooker's side. The pike in it are said to win battles with the swans. Other wildlife on this very natural course includes partridge, pheasant and otter.

Unlike the other two courses, both public property, the Rosemount's early days made it an exclusive preserve of the high gentry. The early membership roll reads like Debrett. Even now visitors should make a reservation in advance by phone or letter giving validation of their club membership. Perhaps curiously the club exercises no discrimination against female members, who enjoy the full privileges of the club's good facilities.

Lone pines are a feature of Rosemount and there used to be one plumb in the middle of the first fairway called the Black Tree. A member living overseas asked that his ashes be scattered under it and rather than submit to the indignity, the pine actually crashed while the ashes were in transit.

St Andrews and the surrounding area is not all golf – but you can visit a local factory to watch clubs being turned out and a museum in the town covers the history of the game. It is also a university town, a seat of learning found-

ed in the 15th-century. The Castle and University are connected by a 'secret' passage open to visitors who will also see the castle's bottle dungeon. Other St Andrews attractions are St Rules Tower and its associated museum.

On sunny days families will need little persuasion to stay close to the resort's golden beaches. The west sands stretch for over a mile, shelving gently into the sea. There are few buildings along the coast road but there is ample parking and the dunes make natural windbreaks for a picnic lunch. East sands have some organised entertainment and the rockpools here can provide hours of enjoyable exploration. An expanding sailing club is based on this side of the town coast and nearby is an open-air seawater swimming pool.

If the skies do darken, take a trip round the many crafts centres of this corner of Fife. See pottery being hand-thrown at Crail, while at Eddergoll Studios (in Cupar) craftsmen perform the intricate leatherwork that goes into the traditional shield called a targe. In St Andrews itself you can take a two-day course in traditional spinning, weaving and macramé at the Loudens Close Workshop.

Perhaps the ideal combination of pursuits on a holiday in this area would be to combine fishing of the Tay or its superb game-filled tributaries with a round or two on the selected courses. This would indeed give you the true flavour of Scotland.

### Angling

River Eden: salmon & trout with fair chances for visitors. Daily tickets: Eden Angling Association (J Fyffe), 67 Braehead, Cupar *Tel: (0334) 3588* Dundee: Crombie Reservoir: fly fishing for trout from boats. Daily tickets: from keeper. Tackle shop: J R Gow, Dundee *Tel: (0382) 25427* River Isla: good trout & grayling. Free fishing beyond Airlie Castle. Further information: Tay Salmon Fisheries Board, Water Bailiff, Alyth *Tel: (082 83) 2329* St Andrews: rock fishing for plaice, flounder & haddock – plus conger by boat. St Andrews Angling Club (D Hutchinson), 25 Swan Street, St Andrews Tayport: good boat fishing for cod, conger, mackerel, mullet, pollack & wrasse

### Camping

Dundee: Camperdown Caravan Site▶▶ *Tel: (0382) 645626* Modern 90-pitch site Open Mar–Sep, must book Jul–Aug South Baldovan Caravan Site▶ *Tel: (0382) 88962* Gently sloping 20-pitch site Open Apr–Oct, must book Jul–Aug Guardbridge: Clayton Milk Bar & Caravan Park ▶▶▶ *Tel: (033 487) 242* Level 75-pitch site (35 tents) 5m NW of St Andrews Open Mar–Oct, must book Jul–Aug Monifieth: Riverview Caravan Park▶▶▶ *Tel: (0382) 23141 ext 413* Grassy 180-pitch site Open Apr–Oct, must book Jul–Aug St Andrews: Craigtown Meadows Holiday Park▶▶▶▶

Tel: (0334) 75959 Well-equipped 90-pitch site Open Mar–Oct, should book Jul–Aug Tayport: East Common Site▶▶ *Tel: (0334) 2334 or 4941* close season Level 100-pitch site (20 caravans) Open Apr–Sep, must book

### General

Arbroath: Kellie Castle: imposing turreted house Open May–Sep daily 10.30–5.30 (ex Tue) Cupar: Hill of Tarvit Mansion House & Garden: remodelled country house with notable tapestries, 2m S of Cupar Open early Apr then May–Sep daily 2–6 (ex Fri – garden open all year 10–dusk Dundee: Barrack St Museum: local shipping & industrial exhibits, plus art & photography Open all year 10–5.30 (ex Sun) *Tel: (0382) 25492 ext 17* Claypotts: unusual 16th-century castle 4m E of Dundee Open all year Mills Observatory: astronomical station equipped with 10in Cooke telescope Open Apr–Sep Mon–Fri 2–7 (2–10 in winter) & Sat 2–5 all year. Spalding Golf Museum: fascinating collection covering three centuries of golf. Open daily (ex Fri & Sun), plus Sun afternoons Easter–Oct Glamis: Angus Folk Museum: row of cottages housing agricultural & domestic items. Open May–Sep daily 1–6 Glamis Castle: royal residence of the Earls of Strathmore, birthplace of HRH Princess Margaret Open May–Oct Mon–Thu & Sun 1–5, plus Fri from Jul

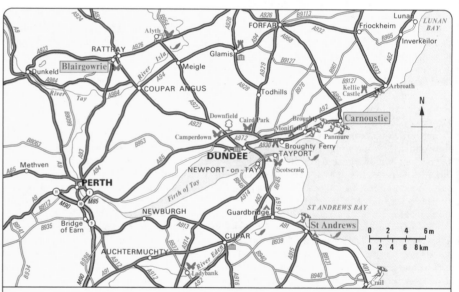

### Alyth
*Tel: (082 83) 268* Breezy moorland course, 18 holes, 6203yds, par 70, SSS70

### Arbroath
*Tel: (0241) 2272* Municipal seaside course, 18 holes, 6078yds, par 70, SSS69 *Professional: G Gellatly*

### Broughty
Links course 6m E of Dundee off A930, 18 holes, 6657yds, par 71, SSS72

### Caird Park (Dundee)
*Tel: (0382) 453606* Parkland course, 18 holes, 6281yds, par 70, SSS70 *Professional: K Todd*

### Camperdown (Dundee)
*Tel: (0382) 645450* Interesting parkland course, 18 holes, 6610yds, par 71, SSS71 *Professional: D Watt*

### Crail
*Tel: (033 35) 278* Very old picturesque course 9m SE of St Andrews, 18 holes, 5749yds, par 69, SSS68

### Downfield (Dundee)
*Tel: (0382) 85595* Rolling woodland course of Championship standard, 18 holes, 6883yds, par 73, SSS73 *Professional: G Hume*

### Ladybank
*Tel: (033 73) 320*

Scenic moorland course 6m SW of Cupar off A914, 18 holes, 6665yds, par 71, SSS72

### Monifieth
*Tel: (082 63) 2767* Two courses, the longer being a Championship course, 18 holes, 6657yds, (5123), par 71 (68), SSS72 (64)

### Panmure
*Tel: (0241) 53120* Testing sandhill course 3m SW of Carnoustie off A930, 18 holes, 6289yds, par 70, SSS7r

### Scotscraig (Tayport)
Tight, but exposed downland course, 18 holes, 6415yds, par 71, SSS71

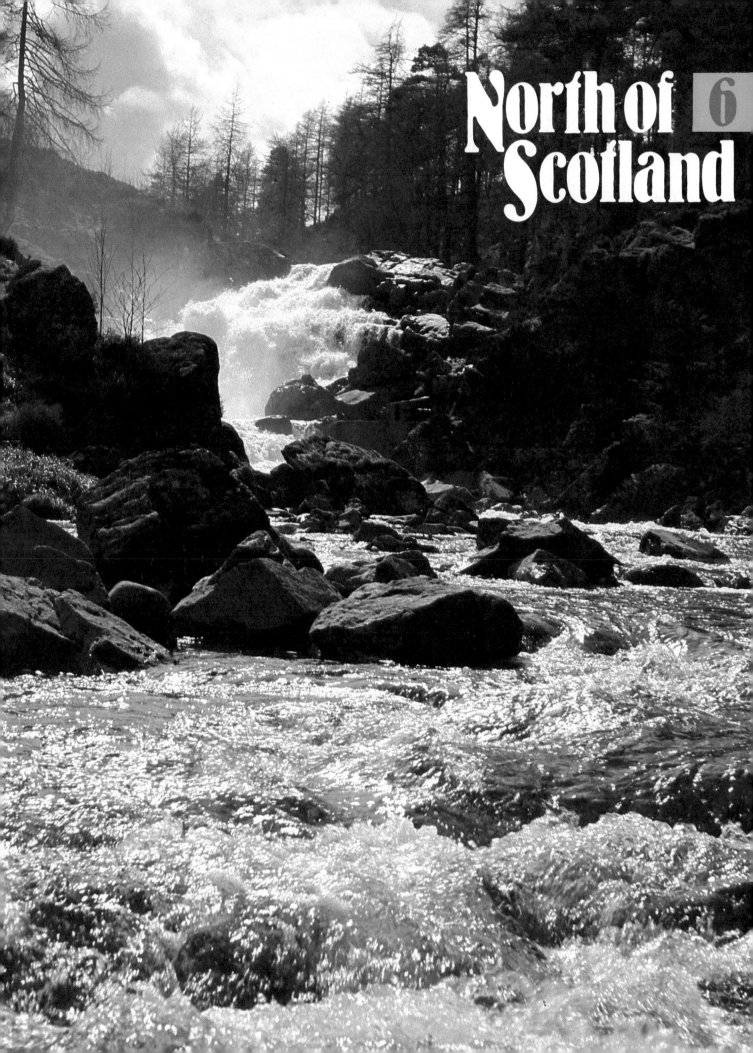

North of Scotland 6

# Royal Dornoch

Royal Dornoch, Golf Road,
Dornoch, Sutherland
*Tel: Dornoch (086 281) 219*

Take A949 off main A9 coast road

Links course: 6533yds, SSS72
*Course designer:* Tom Morris Senior

Visitors welcome at most times
*Professional:* W Skinner

Hotels: Burghfield House★★ Dornoch
*Tel: Dornoch (086 281) 212*

Dornoch★★ Dornoch
*Tel: Dornoch (086 281) 351*
(107 rm)

Dornoch Castle★★ Dornoch
*Tel: Dornoch (086 281) 216*
(21 rm)

Royal Golf★★★ Dornoch
*Tel: Dornoch (086 281) 283*

While Thurso may lay claim to the title of the most northerly golf course on the British mainland (to set the record straight, the Shetlands boast a course and the Orkneys have three), Royal Dornoch is the furthest north that the Scottish Championship has ever ventured. Poised at the mouth of that last great bite out of Scotland's east coast, the Dornoch Firth, this ancient burgh has yielded some of the earliest references to golf in the sport's long history.

Dornoch was given royal title in 1628 by that golfing monarch Charles I, so it can be safely assumed that the game was played on the superb links land near to the town for some years prior to that date. It is surprising, then, that the foundation of the golf club as we know it today was delayed until 1877, to receive its own royal title from Edward VII in 1906. Much of the history of the game in the area is recorded in the archives of the old county of Sutherland, of which Dornoch was the county town. These are still held in Dunrobin Castle.

There is an old-world tranquillity about the town itself – properly it is called a city, since there is a cathedral which was burnt down in 1570. Today's building was rebuilt some two centuries later but a local hotel incorporates parts of the old central tower of the original Bishop's Palace. An Irish monk who became St Finnibar converted the people in this region long before the ravaging Norsemen arrived and some say his whimsical influences still preside over the golf club. Certainly he controls the weather, which is unusually kindly for this northern location – as the locals say, 'the blaw is usually mild.'

There are other amusing diversions at Royal Dornoch. In a cottage garden, a commemorative stone marks the spot where the last Scottish witch was burned. Before Janet Horne was tied to the stake she was tossed into a pond that now forms part of the golf course – the nearby hole is popularly known as 'The Witch'. She was not the only thing to be dunked here – the water also conceals a German field-gun presented to the burgh by a grateful War Department. Perched elegantly on a brae, it was one night the focus of some golfers' revels and rolled down the slope to sink without trace.

Sons of Dornoch are strong-minded individualists. There was a rule at the club that no 4-balls should start before 11.30am. When Prime Minister Asquith came for a golfing holiday, he asked if the rule could be waived for himself and some friends. They had to conform like the rest and when, subsequently, the match got underway, a posse of women waylaid the players, pelting them with vegetables and shouting 'Votes for women!'.

A holiday home overlooking the second hole was used by Joyce (later Lady Heathcoat Amory) and Roger Wethered, the great champions who learned their golf here. From their window they could see luckless players throwing their balls free of the large sand bunker shored up by railway sleepers that used

to be on the course. Several such hazards were removed from Royal Dornoch after a caddie was killed by a rebounding ball.

The main Championship High Links (there is also a short overflow course) at Royal Dornoch has a similar standard of excellence to St Andrews, Carnoustie and Troon. Tom Morris senior was largely responsible for the early layout but, as at other great Scottish courses, nature was the main architect. Strung along the shore on sand-based turf, the course strays up and down a gorse-topped ridge. Fairways have whins and burns and many of the greens are on shallow plateaux. Little inlets of the sea characterise many holes and the sandy sub-soil guarantees that water never stays for long on the green surfaces.

From the start, the difficulties of Dornoch are all too apparent. To make a ball stay on the green is a feat of considerable dexterity. Hole 2 is as difficult a par 3 as one meets anywhere, with deep traps drawing your ball to either side of the green. Your caddie will tell you the white cottage in view is 'Grannie's Hielan' Hame', that of the song. The course tumbles off the

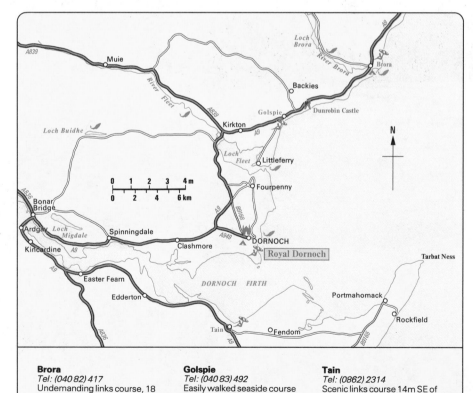

**Brora**
*Tel: (040 82) 417*
Undemanding links course, 18 holes, 6110yds, par 69, SSS69

**Golspie**
*Tel: (040 83) 492*
Easily walked seaside course between Dornoch & Brora off A9, 18 holes, 5852yds, par 69, SSS68

**Tain**
*Tel: (0862) 2314*
Scenic links course 14m SE of Kincardine off A9, 18 holes, 6207yds, par 70, SSS70

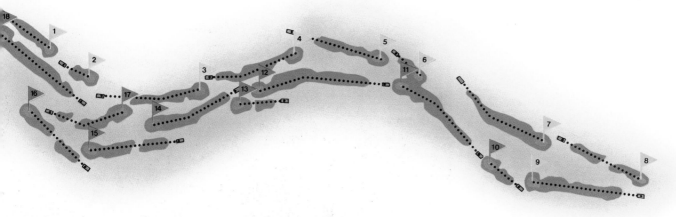

*Dunrobin Castle, Golspie*

escarpment on to the foreshore for hole 3, with the green on a well-guarded plateau. The 4th and the 14th have been nominated by Donald Ross as two of the finest par 4s in the world – hole 4 follows the contour line of the sand bluff and 14, in the opposite direction has no bunkers at all, the ground is quite enough.

However mild the weather may be in general, it has to be said that the occasional gale can whip across the links with great venom. A local postmaster, nicknamed 'Tosh', said that once on the 165-yard par 3 6th, his ball was blown off course, and even off the green, so often that the card was marked at 13 and he had not played a bad shot among them!

Tipping over the edge again on the 8th, you actually tee off on the line of the white cottage and hope to find the pearl of the green lying in a saucer-shaped hollow between dunes with your second. The turn into the wind for the 9th and the homeward leg leaves eight more holes of splendid golf before you can claim your home-baked scones in the clubhouse.

Dornoch has extensive clean and sandy beaches, both to the south of the town on the links shore and to the north at Embo (scene of a 1248 battle in which Bishop Gilbert was slain by Danish invaders). The shore has a gentle slope but quite the best bathing area is just south of the rocks close to the car park and beach shelter.

The town makes a good touring centre for the whole of the Highland's west coast up to the promontory of John o' Groats. It is a picturesque coastline dotted with small fishing ports such as Helmsdale where, despite the fall-off of catches, fishermen can be seen handling their live cargo of lobsters taken in the comparatively deep inshore waters. Nearby, Brora has its own rolling links course set out by James Braid and this is close to a small campsite which is separated from the beach by a low dune bank. Golspie, just north of Embo is a very quiet holiday resort, its broad beach dotted with sheltering rocks.

On the slopes of Ben Bhraggie, behind Golspie, is a statue to the 1st Duke of Sutherland. He was an immensely rich man whose only claim to infamy is that he was responsible for the Highland Clearances programme which

rekindled Scottish hatred of the English in the 19th-century. A well-trodden footpath skirting Golspie and taking in the slopes of Ben Bhraggie gives superb views of the Dornoch Firth and the surrounding hills.

The Dornoch Firth is a fine sea angling area. While there is rock fishing at Embo and several shore marks for beach casting, many anglers prefer to get afloat in boats from Brora, Embo and by arrangement from the management of the Grannie's Heilan' Hame campsite (who also arrange sea trout spinning). As well as this site, which has impressive facilities, you can also camp at the Royal Dornoch Links site not, despite its name, actually on the course. It is, however, close enough to make the combination of golf and camping a fine holiday choice.

**Angling**
Brora: rock & shore fishing for codling, mullet & plaice. Plus cod, haddock & skate by boat
River Brora: fly fishing only for good trout & salmon
Daily tickets (from riparian owner in advance): The Factor, Sutherland Estates, Golspie
*Tel: (040 83) 268*
Loch Buidhe: fly fishing for trout (residents of Burghfield House Hotel, Dornoch only)
Dornoch: shore fishing for bass, flatfish, mackerel & pollack. Plus possible cod & tope by boat
River Fleet: small stream with large estuary, fair salmon & sea trout
Daily tickets (in advance): J Baddon, Golspie
*Tel: (040 83) 212*
Little Ferry: 3m stream at Dornoch with good sea trout
Daily tickets (in advance):
W A Macdonald, Castle Street, Dornoch
*Tel: (086 281) 301*

**Camping**
Brora: Riverside Caravan Site ▶

*Tel: (040 82) 353*
Partly sloping 21-pitch site (6 caravans)
Open May–Sep, no bookings
Dornoch: Grannie's Heilan Home ▶▶▶▶
*Tel: (086 281) 260*
Coastal 325-pitch site (100 tents)
Open Jun–Aug, no bookings
Royal Dornoch Links Caravan & Camping Site ▶▶▶
*Tel: (086 281) 423 – or (040 83) 392*
Nov–Mar
Level 160-pitch woodland site
Open mid-Apr–Oct, should book Jul–Aug

**General**
Dornoch: Dornoch Cathedral: restored 13th-century church, an impressive landmark. Accessible at all times.
Information Centre: Sutherland Tourist Organisation, The Square
*Tel: (086 281) 400*
Golspie: Dunrobin Castle: home of the Earls & Dukes of Sutherland, with small museum & beautiful gardens
Open May–Sep daily 10.30–5.30 (Sun afternoons only)
*Tel: (040 83) 377*

# Nairn

Nairn Golf Club, Seabank Road,
Nairn, Highland
*Tel: Nairn (0667) 53208*

West of town off A96 (well signposted)

Links course: 6544yds, SSS71
Designed by Archie Simpson and
modified by Tom Morris and James
Braid

Visitors welcome, reservations
advisable
*Professional:* G McKintosh

Hotels: Golf View★★★★ Nairn
*Tel: Nairn (0667) 52301*
(57 rm)

Newton★★★★ Nairn
*Tel: Nairn (0667) 53144*
(31 rm)

Royal Marine★★★ Nairn
*Tel: Nairn (0667) 53381*
(43 rm)

Windsor★★ Nairn
*Tel: Nairn (0667) 53108*
(48 rm)

Like Gullane and North Berwick, Nairn's niche on the coastline of the Moray Firth's south shore is threatened by coastal erosion. In fact, about twenty-five years ago, a storm and an exceptionally high tide robbed the Nairn club, one mile west of the town, of fifty to sixty yards of its turf and overnight improved some of the hazards that James Braid laid down during his heyday as a golf champion and architect. The sea is now within a whisker of five of the first six holes and on the fifth the Moray Firth presents an intriguing problem to habitual slicers.

Nairn is quite a youngster in Scottish Club terms, being founded in 1887 on first class links land close to a sandy shore. It was very rough ground marched over by heather and gorse, representing a considerable challenge to

the club's first architect, Archie Simpson. In fact it is said that Simpson's design did not please the council, who called for that grand old man of golf, Tom Morris Senior to sort things out. Even his administrations were only enjoyed until Braid came along to give the course something of its present form.

Nairn is known as a liberal club, with some pioneering firsts to its name. The club claims to have been the pioneer of golf package holidays. The Nairn Golf Week includes instruction seminars, unlimited play on the course and the attention of professionals of the calibre of Dai Rees at an all-inclusive price. It was at Nairn that spectator gate money was charged for the first time – crowds flocked to see an 1899 exhibition match by Open Champion Harry Vardon, who played for the then princely sum of £15.

Nairn's position on the south shore of the Moray Firth means that it is sheltered more than most courses on this coast from the terrible fury of the North Sea winds. For a links

land so close to the sea, it is unusual in showing those seasonal change of colours in its gorse and heather cover that more often characterise an inland heath. From many of the tees and greens there are background views of the Black Isle and the mountains of Ross and Sutherland across the water.

Nairn's course runs east-west with the first seven holes being played along the shoreline into the prevailing wind. The first hole holds no terrors at all, par 4 should be easily attainable over its 401-yard length, provided you are not intimidated by the sea. At the second tee, you are no more than a long putt from the beach, although you should have no problem in clearing the mouth of a burn as it spills into the sea across the fairway.

The sea is left behind you on the 377-yard dogleg of the 3rd – but not for long. On the short 4th, you drive directly to the sea over a large dune to the part of the shore that was most affected by erosion. Put anything to the left of the green and you are perilously close to

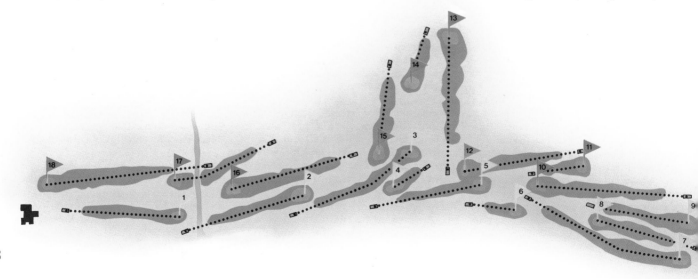

*Inverness Castle*

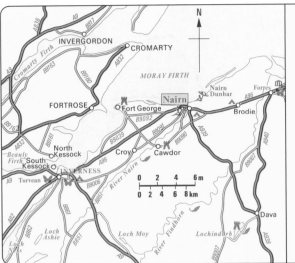

the beach. Now the ground has been cut away, the 5th is one of the most testing holes, although a great bunker placed by Braid to the left will eat players who shy from taking the straight course along the sea's edge. The green has two tiers to be negotiated.

The 8th, with its awkward plateau green winds back in the opposite direction to the shoreside holes but does not, in fact, mark the turn, as the 9th is a parallel turn-about. On the home leg you must conquer the 500-yard 10th, Nairn's second longest hole, and come to grips with the testing 12th. Gorse crowds in each side of the fairway and keeping the ball running true down the middle will give many visitors pause for thought. Immediately afterwards you face direct south for the 13th which takes players for a deviation inland and a fresh set of problems. With the sun in your eyes you may not at first define the clever little bunkers let into the gorse that lines the bumpy fairway. This hole terminates in a classic pulpit green with some bemusing slants to it.

Play levels off to the home hole (the longest of all) with the sea constantly in view as you approach the parasol pines of the 17th and a tricky second shot to clear the burn guarding the green approach.

Nairn also has the 9-hole Newton Course, a favourite of the club's lady members and often the holiday relaxation of Harold Macmillan and Lady Dorothy who number among the club's more illustrious visitors. The layout of this course is on a slightly higher plateau than the main links, with fine views across the water. A reminder that both courses can be exposed to some wretched weather is entombed in a 1907 rule of the Nairn club – 'That ladies be allowed to take lunch and tea *inside* the clubhouse when the thermometer reaches freezing point'. Happily Nairn is a little more liberated these days.

The town of Nairn, only eighteen miles from Inverness, is distinguished today by the fact that it has two four-star hotels, unusual for its size. Of these, both the Golf View and the Newton cater for touring golfers. Nairn's beaches of golden sand are a magnet to families from all over Scotland and it is no brash resort – many people come here for the very wide range of outdoor activities provided.

Around the East Beach there are canoes, fishing dinghies and fishing tackle for hire and facilities for snorkelling, diving, water-ski-ing and pleasure boat trips around the waters of the Moray Firth. Sea fishing along this coast is superb. While in Nairn itself there are favoured spots on the two piers at the harbour entrance. There is a lot more action on the coast to the east and at Lossiemouth, where sea trout are taken by spinning into the breakers.

Lossiemouth is a local centre for commercial fishing boats and it is a thriving town with some attractive buildings in the cluster of 17th-century houses that forms its heart. This was Ramsey MacDonald's home town and his birthplace is marked by a plaque. The village of Findhorn which lies between Nairn and Lossiemouth has had a chequered history. Today's settlement is the third to be founded in the area after sandstorms wiped out the original 17th-century village – a flood destroyed a second set of houses only sixty years later.

For campers, this sheltered shore has many havens with sites strung along the coast from Inverness itself through Nairn to Lossiemouth.

Inverness is sure to lure families away from golf for at least a day. Situated close to the mouth of the River Ness and the Caledonian Canal, Inverness is very much the regional centre of the Highland area, with an important part to play in the survival of Gaelic culture. It has also been an important military centre with a number of links to the campaigns of Cromwell and General Wade. Just three miles east of the town is the battlefield of Culloden, where Bonnie Prince Charlie's hopes of restoring the Stuart monarchy were cruelly dashed by the Duke of Cumberland. The battlefield is today a beautiful place to walk over, having well-marked history and natural history trails and a fascinating visitor centre portraying some

dramatic scenes from the conflict of 1746.

Nairn is good central base for tours of the whole of this area and forays deeper inland to the mountain refuges of the Cairngorms. Nairn golf course is not the only place for the sport in the area either. On the other side of town is the 18-hole Dunbar links course and at Inverness it is said that they have more left-handed players than anywhere else in the world – a product perhaps of the Highland addiction to that vicious sport 'shinty' (a particularly Scottish variety of hockey).

# Pitlochry

Pitlochry Estates Office, Pitlochry,
Perthshire, Tayside
*Tel: Pitlochry (0796) 2114*

On A9

Attractive wooded course with fine
views: 5811yds, SSS68
*Course designer:* Major Cecil
Hutchinson

Visitors welcome particularly if
telephoned first
*Professional:* J Wilson

Hotels: Burnside★★ Pitlochry
*Tel: Pitlochry (0796) 2203*
(6 rm)

Green Park★★★ Pitlochry
*Tel: Pitlochry (0796) 2537*
(37 rm)

Pine Trees★★★ Pitlochry
*Tel: Pitlochry (0796) 2121*
(18 rm)

**Aberfeldy**
*Tel: (088 72) 535*
Course close River Tay, 9 holes,
5466yds, par 68, SSS67

**Blair Atholl**
Course alongside river, 9 holes,
5718yds, par 70, SSS69

**Dunkeld and Birnham**
*Tel: (035 02) 524*
Heathland course, ½m N of
Dunkeld off A9, 9 holes, 5264yds,
par 68, SSS68

**Taymouth Castle**
*Tel: (088 73) 228*
Parkland course in castle
grounds, 6m W of Aberfeldy, 18
holes, 6087yds, par 69, SSS69

Deep in Tayside and close to Scotland's geographical centre, is the beautiful summer resort of Pitlochry, a town set in the wooded valley of the River Tummel, a major Tay tributary and salmon haunt. Dammed near the town to form Loch Faskally, the river in this area is a source of hydro-electric power. There are many small hotels with attractive views of the loch and the surrounding Grampian hills and the town has gained a reputation as a cultural centre particularly for the Pitlochry Festival Theatre.

Loch Faskally actually submerged the town's original nine-hole golf course but there was no way in which the town would accept a break with its long history of golf and a new course was inaugurated in 1909. The brassie with which Colonel C A J Butter drove the first shot on the new grounds laid out by Major Cecil Hutchinson is displayed in the professional's shop. The Colonel's family still controls the club as part of its land holdings.

The designer had to contend with as devious a set of natural obstacles as on any highland course. The moorland contours heave up and down, interspersed with woods and the result is that there is *always* a breathtaking view.

The first holes are a comparatively steep zig-zag upward but from the 4th the course is less physically demanding and players can concentrate more on the skills required to negotiate Pitlochry's considerable undulations. Three fascinating short holes at the 7th, 11th and 16th are features of this mountain test which has no par 5. This does not mean, however that 4s can be expected at every hole. For example, the tee shot at the 14th, named 'Tulloch', has a line lying between sentinel birch trees and a very slippery green.

For golfing historians every Pitlochry hole is a thrill. Climbing up the first fairway is a track once used by Bonnie Prince Charlie and his army of Highlanders. Mary Queen of Scots rested to pluck her harp on the spot that is the 5th green. Druids worshipped at the 6th and the tee of the 7th is laid over the remains of a Pictish fort, a place from which King Bruce surveyed the valley after the battle of Methven. At the 16th there was a whisky distillery.

There are no playing restrictions at this delightfully friendly club, which annually entertains holidaying players from all over the country in the high jinks of the Highland Golf Week held every August. Great Scottish golfers such as Bobby Cruikshank, Tommy Armour, Eric Brown and John Panton played the Highland while amateurs. In this company it is good to know that the course record has been held for over twenty years by golfing parson Reverend W P Henderson. The course is relatively short at about 5800 yards and the par is just 68 but Henderson's 65 has only been equalled twice. Max Faulkner played Pitlochry, too. In a Cancer Research charity exhibition a spectator challenged him to jump the deep ten-foot wide burn guarding the 18th green for a £2 donation. Faulkner accepted, took a running jump and just failed to make it – he sat up in the muddy water grinning, his glamour golf gear ruined.

If you are not out walking the course, the Pitlochry area offers several other splendid opportunities to stretch the legs. There are forest trails in the woods around Dunkeld, Aberfeldy, Kenmore and Pitlochry itself, with leaflets available from local Forestry Commission offices. If hotel accommodation is not for you there are beautiful campsites at Blair Atholl, Tummel Bridge, Glengoulandie and Aberfeldy, with two at Pitlochry.

**Angling**
Loch Bhac: fly fishing
for trout from bank
near Pitlochry
Daily tickets:
Pitlochry Angling
Club, c/o Pitlochry
Tourist Office, 28
Atholl Road, Pitlochry
*Tel: (0796) 2215*
River Braan: trout
stream
Daily tickets:
Amulree Hotel,
Amulree
*Tel: (035 05) 218*
Butterstone Loch: fly
fishing for trout near
Dunkeld
Daily tickets
(keeper): Lochend
Cottage
Loch Faskally:
salmon plus fly
fishing for trout
Daily tickets: P D
Malloch, 83 Atholl
Road, Pitlochry
*Tel: (0796) 2228*
River Tay: salmon,
trout & coarse fishing
Daily tickets:
Dunkeld House
Hotel, Dunkeld;
Grantully Castle
Estate Office,
Grantully,
Aberfeldy; Loch Tay
Guest House,
Kenmore

**Camping**
Aberfeldy: Municipal
Caravan Site ►►
*Tel: (035 02) 662*
Level grass site, 120
pitches
Open Mar–Oct, no
bookings
Birnham: Erigmore

House caravan
Park ►►►►
*Tel: (035 02) 236*
Flattish 80-pitch site
Open Apr–Oct, no
bookings
Pitlochry: Faskally
Home Farm ►►►
*Tel: (0796) 2007*
Grassland site near
river, 400 pitches
Open Easter–Oct,
must book

**General**
Blair Atholl: Blair
Castle: 13th-century
origin with 18th-
century alterations
Open Easter, then
May–Oct daily
Dunkeld: Loch of
Lowes Wild Life
Reserve: rare
wildfowl plus indoor
exhibition
Open Apr–Sep daily
*Tel: (035 02) 337 or
267 off season*
Killiecrankie: Trust
Visitor Centre: close
to site of 1689 battle
where 'Bonnie
Dundee' rousted
King William's troops
Open Apr–Sep
Pitlochry: Pitlochry
Power Station, Dam
& Fish Pass: hydro-
electricity exhibition
Open Easter–Oct
Queen's View:
Tummel Forest
Centre: exhibition
showing changes
since Queen
Victoria's time, plus
forest walks and
picnic areas
Open Easter–Sep